WHERE EAGLES HARE

Thomas Carnihan

Published

by

Where Eagles Hare

This Edition published in 2013

Text and Design Where Eagles Hare

ISBN 978-0-9926885-0-9

Photography: Thomas Carnihan   Cover Design: Thomas Carnihan   Design and Layout: Thomas Carnihan

Graphic and Technical Consultant: Bob Watkins

Editor: Teresa Akgunduz

Printed by

WHERE EAGLES HARE

INTRODUCTION

This book is all about one man's passion to train a Golden Eagle to catch a Slovakian hare.

Slovakian Hares are notoriously difficult to catch as they are hunted on by wild eagles, and there isn't a trick in the book that they haven't learnt about avoiding capture.

Hopefully my photos will illustrate this point.

The Slovakian hares can weigh as much as five thousand grams, whereas English brown hares average around three thousand six hundred grams. It was a goal that took me almost eight years to achieve.

I had no idea at the time how much this would cost me, not in terms of money but how my life was to change for ever. Whilst writing this book my marriage of some 34 years, to my childhood sweetheart broke up. This is something I bitterly regret every day since. However I had a wonderful time during those 34 years and have subsequently dug down deep to continue on my own. I have flown, trained and bred many different species of birds of prey.

From where it all started

I'm self-taught although I had a wonderful and kind mentor by the name of Philip Samuel Dugmore. He taught me so much about captive breeding and with his lovely wife Pauline, were some of the most knowledgeable people I have ever met.

So this book is not about teaching others how to train eagles. I borrowed Philip Glazier's book 'Falconry and Hawking' when I started way back in the seventies and this served me well throughout the years that I hunted with Hawks and Falcons. If you have been practising falconry for ten years or more you won't need a book, and if you have been doing falconry for less than ten years you won't be ready for a Golden Eagle.

Golden Eagles are not for the faint hearted or foolhardy and can be extremely aggressive, and downright dangerous if not handled and trained correctly. It takes talent, a great deal of common sense and a minimum of at least ten years falconry experience, to train and hunt with one.

Recently there have been incidents of Harris Hawks being incorrectly trained and attacking small dogs belonging to members of the public.

It would only take one or two such incidents with Golden Eagles to attract enough publicity to have them listed under the Dangerous Wild Animals Act. There are now several well organised groups of eagle falconers in the UK, who go about their sport in a manner that has to be applauded and only allow experienced eagle falconers to join them. It's not elitist, but there is an enormous amount of responsibility not to bring the sport of falconry into disrepute.

Over the last five or six years I have taken up photography. When my mother died she left me a small amount of money and I thought it would be a really nice idea to use it to buy a camera, so every time I took a good photo I would remember her. The camera cost less than a hundred pounds but it took one of my most famous sets of photographs of a blue hare being caught by a Harris Hawk, high up in the Cairngorm Mountains.

This book is all about Kaiser, my eagle but I have also included lots of action photos of other falconers, hawks and eagles.

My camera has since been upgraded but that set of photos has gone six times round the world and every time I see them somewhere, I remember my mother with fond affection.

Hopefully the photos in the book will be a major talking point. I know little about photography I just point and shoot, however I suspect I will be remembered more for my photos than my life-long, knowledge and love of falconry and hunting with eagles. Those that have written before me, about Golden Eagles, have often said that their use as falconry birds is much undervalued. Times have moved on and we are beginning to catch up with our European friends, and eagle meetings in the UK are proving extremely popular. I have hunted in the UK with Kaiser at many eagle meets including organising a number myself.

Hunting with eagles has become a passion for me and a way of life, it's in your blood. I've spoken to many of my friends who hunt with eagles and they all say the same thing.

"....extreme hawking at its best."

You live and breathe it and from the minute you see your first Golden Eagle you want one and nothing will get in your way. I have never ever lost any enthusiasm from the day I first saw a Golden Eagle hunting till today, some thirty five years on. I always get a real rush of adrenalin when I'm taking Kaiser out hunting, something I'll never lose, it's infectious. To watch eagles hunting is just breath-taking.

The minute the eagle leaves your fist in pursuit of its quarry you're the spectator, witnessing nature at its best. It's not about killing things, we are sportsmen. Numbers don't mean anything; if we wanted to come home with a dozen hares we could buy a gun. As said, this is nature at its best, there are no better equals. The hare, or as I prefer to call them 'Houdinis' are magicians, they have an uncanny arsenal of tricks up their sleeve when it comes to evading capture from a hunting eagle.

To watch a hare react knowing it is seconds away from capture is amazing, you can never predict what it is going to do next. Despite running at forty miles an hour they can come to a immediate stop.

They can change direction in less than a split second to face the hunter head on only to then leap clean over the predator and make their escape, through the air, with a dazzling display of aerobatics that would put most gymnasts to shame. Or they can jink left or right or stop dead in the blink of an eye, and again make the hunter look completely foolish. I'm so pleased, over the years, that I took my camera out with me. Sometimes Kaiser could go days if not weeks without catching a hare, but I have captured the proof of why this is such a wonderful sport. My photos illustrate, only too well, how difficult hares are to catch. I never get upset if he doesn't catch one especially as Kaiser has an almost impossible handicap. In time he came to understand that to catch hares he has to use his brains as well as his power and speed proving over the years he has learnt well taking some spectacular hares. Kaiser has caught deer but nothing adds to the excitement of a good eagle coursing a hare, the hunter and the hunted on equal terms, extreme hawking at its best.

If this book is a success then maybe I will go back to the beginning and write a book about how I got my first falcon.

"These damn things keep following me everywhere, can't get away from them!"

My next book starts at the beginning ………...

"The picture that springs to mind, going back thirty years or so, I am sitting in a 'Mark 3' Escort estate car, wearing a pin striped suit. It's my lunch hour, the home-made cheese and onion sandwiches are a much needed, long awaited sustenance. I look across at a recreational park in Corby, my mind momentarily escaping from thoughts of my job as a chemical analyst for a water treatment company.

My gaze is focused on a young lad, Don Mckye, walking towards the park swinging what appeared to be an old shoe. I found out later that the shoe was in fact a lure, and was being swung around the lad's head attracting six juvenile Kestrels flying thirty feet above, all screaming their heads off. I was transfixed for the next twenty minutes, watching in utter amazement. I grew up in the countryside and my father's friends bringing him baby foxes, hares, stoats or swans with a variety of injuries for treatment were commonplace. But here, before me was a spectacle like which I had never seen before. A lad with half a dozen wild young kestrels following his every command. They were stooping at the lure with such enthusiasm, and for the next twenty minutes he had them hooked (me as well) chasing this tired looking bit of old leather shoe with a piece of meat attached to it. Every now and then he would let a kestrel take the lure and settle on the ground to reap his reward, only to be quickly followed by his brothers and sisters all wanting their piece of the action.

Fascinated, I got out of the car and approached this now very nervous looking young lad. He was wary of a bloke in a pin striped suit, looking official.

His words still echo in my memories…

"Hey, are you the RSPCA? I'm glad you've come. These damn things keep following me everywhere, can't get away from them! They live on top of the house and every time I come out they follow me." He laughed nervously!

I said "I hate the RSPCA, but would you sell me one of them kestrels they're awesome?"

"Phew! That's a relief, thought you were gonna nick me. Yes, you can have one for thirty quid." (In 1977 that was a lot of money for an eagle let alone some nicked un-rung Kestrel) Before he had the chance to change his mind, I emptied my pockets and offered him all the money I had on me.

"£25.00 that's all I've got?"

"ok, you can owe me the rest!"

I recall getting home and my ex-wife being aghast at what I'd brought with me this time! Typical woman, I got interrogated, I relayed the story and that it cost me thirty quid, but I owed the guy because I only had £25.00 on me. Exasperated, she pointed out that the money was for our shopping for the next week! "Don't worry," I calmly replied, "he will be catching rabbits by the end of the week once I've trained him."

The very next day I went into the local library and permanently borrowed 'Falconry and Hawking' by Philip Glazier. I hadn't got any money left to buy the book, but this book was my introduction to falconry and became my Bible for the next thirty years.

I called the Kestrel Kes, as in the film and although today I have Kaiser, it was Kes that started it all. Buying him was the most amazing thing I have ever done in my life. From the day I bought him he was never out of my sight. I was totally besotted by this beautiful little feathered friend that was to be my companion for the next sixteen years. He never did catch a rabbit!

Several weeks later I saw the lad again and told him that Glazier's book said that Kestrels don't catch rabbits, so he sold me a buzzard, explaining that this one catches hares and foxes as well. I'm a glutton for punishment; it was probably the noisiest bird in the world. Day and night it would scream its head off and only ever caught worms! Here was sown the seeds of my divorce some thirty years on!

Anyway Kes was here to stay, where I went he went, never out of my sight day or night, living in the lounge most of the time. I was so nuts about this little creature that my life changed for ever. Fishing rods, cars, model planes, everything went out of the window, Kes took my total attention. Nothing was too good for this little fellow.

So that's where the story starts. I had that kestrel for sixteen years before my 'charming' little Patterdale Fell Terrier bit his head off! It took 3 years for my wife to tell me what had happened otherwise I would have killed the dog! If one can ever judge oneself then I measure my achievements by how long this little fellow stayed my companion, free flying for some sixteen years over the skies of Great Houghton…………"

This drawing of Kes, by Mark Thacker and the literature that it accompanied adorned the middle pages of the Observer on the 16th of September 1990

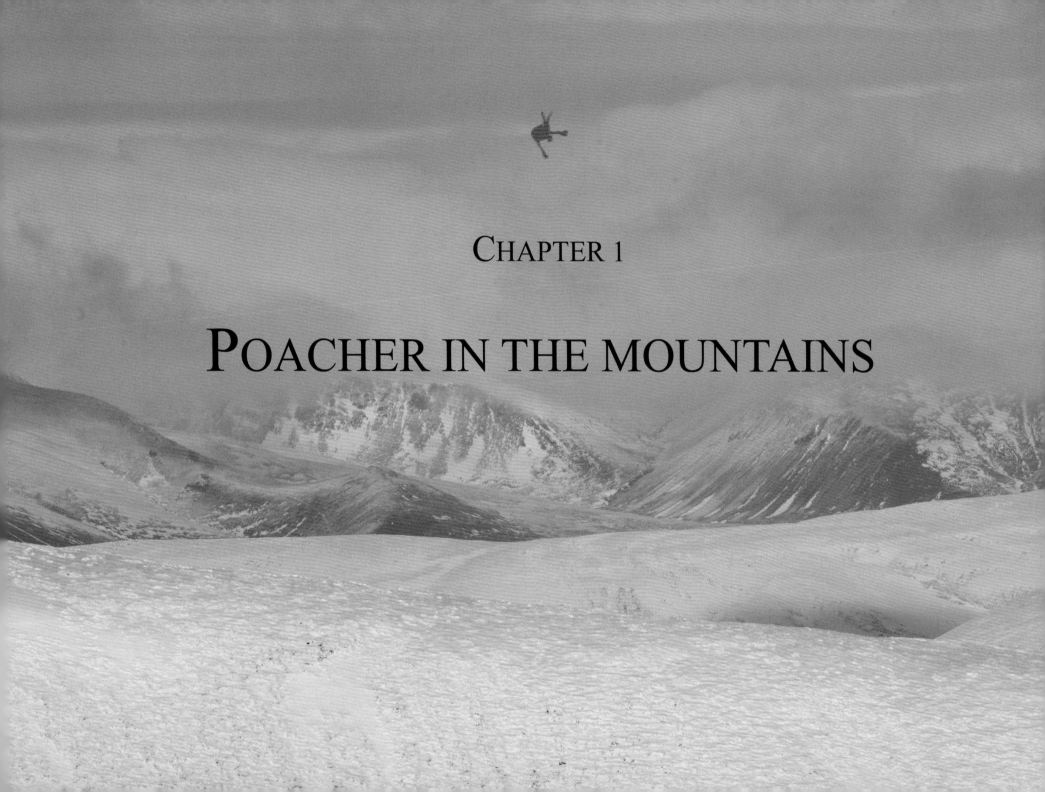

CHAPTER 1

POACHER IN THE MOUNTAINS

My Love of eagles goes way back to the early seventies when I had several African Tawny Eagles, all bred by my Mentor Philip Dugmore and his wife Pauline. Over the years we became great friends, Philip and Pauline have been one of the finest breeders of raptors the UK has ever had. They taught me everything I ever needed to know about breeding raptors. I used the eagles mostly for display work; however some showed great promise as hunting birds.

In the early eighties I was asked if I would be willing to do a film commercial for Nordica Ski Boots, by an Italian TV production company called Gruppo Cooper. They wanted me to take my Tawny Eagle up into the Alps in Northern Italy on the border with Switzerland. It was a place called Zermatt Plateau Rosa, in the Aosta Valley, on Piccolo Cervino 3,883 metres above sea level.

The brief was that an eagle was to soar as high as it could then stoop down from a 1000ft and land onto a red ski boot! I was up for it. The boss of the Italian company flew over to England with some photographers and did a photo shoot of the eagle just to make sure the colour of my Tawny was acceptable to Nordica Ski Boots. All the final details where sorted, fee, flights, insurance etc. I was given ten weeks to get the eagle fit and sort out all the necessary paperwork.

The following weekend I was doing a display in the field at the back of our house. No travelling expenses for this display! The farmer, Rolly Evans, was putting on a small country fair with the emphasis on sheep dog trials and I agreed to put on a free display, in gratitude for allowing me to fly my birds on his land. The country fair had lots of visitors it was a lovely summer's day with clear blue skies, we had a good display of birds on show. All was going well when disaster struck. I was flying the Tawny Eagle in the ring, it was about sixty feet up in the air, about a hundred and fifty yards away, I was calling him back to the fist, when out of the corner of my eye I saw a very young child run from his mother across the flying arena.

The toddler had an ice cream in his hand and as I was feeding the eagle on white rats I didn't want the eagle flying down and grabbing the ice cream by mistake.

Immediately I put my hand down, telling the eagle to fly round again in another circle, allowing time for the child to get across the ring to safety. Unfortunately the eagle decided not to fly round again, but to go and land on an electricity pylon next to the ring. This was disastrous; he got caught up in the wires and was electrocuted immediately. It was horrific to watch and there was a large crowd of spectators, all distressed at the sight. The eagle was hanging upside down for some considerable time before falling to the ground. I was stunned to see such a beautiful bird die in this way. By the time I picked up the eagle he was already dead and there was nothing I could do. I was devastated!

It wasn't until a couple of days later I remembered I still had a contract with Gruppo Cooper to fly a Tawny Eagle in the Alps for them. Tawny Eagles were fetching around £2000 at the time and that particular eagle was called Access as I purchased him on a credit card. I didn't have the money to go out and buy another one. I was in a dilemma and didn't know what to do when my life-long best friend, Dick smith who was watching the display a few days earlier, called round and said come on Tommy lets go for a drive. I asked him where we were going, but he just told me to shut up and get in the car. With Dick you learn to just go with the flow and don't ask questions. We drove for about 3 hours or so and arrived in Gateshead, I still didn't have a clue what was going on. We stopped at a house and Dick knocked at the front door.

A very large guy came out and said "You must be Tom and Dick." Dick replied "Yes, I'm sorry we couldn't bring Harry Ha Ha! You must be Hugh Haggerty!" I knew the name immediately, as a breeder of birds of prey. I still didn't have a clue as to why we were here, but followed them through the house to the back garden, where I spotted a very large Tawny Eagle sitting on a bow perch. Dick asked what I thought of him but I wasn't sure what he meant. He pointed at the Tawny Eagle asking if I would be able to fool the Italians into thinking it was the same Tawny Eagle that had been electrocuted the previous weekend.

I explained that the colour was similar and I could also say it had moulted since they saw it last!

It was a fabulous looking Tawny Eagle, and I guessed that it had been bred by Phil Dugmore. I was right and Hugh explained that it was related to the one that had just died. Dick asked if he had a box we could put it in and Hugh went to fetch one. I was still confused; I didn't have the money to buy the eagle! Dick said he would buy it for me and I could pay him back later. "Bloody hell! Dick, Are you sure? I'm still paying for the other one on my credit card for the next three years." He told me to put the eagle in the box and we'd sort the money out another time. Dick is such an amazing guy, we have had our ups and downs over the years but Dick being a true friend had rang round to find another Tawny Eagle for me so I could still do the film work in Italy. So we parted with £2000, well Dick did, thanked Hugh and made our way back home.

Poacher, The Tawny Eagle just before we flew to Italy.

I called the eagle Poacher and the next day set about training him , well away from any pylons, lesson learnt! Within a week or so I was back on track. I sold the dead Tawny Eagle for £1000 to Martin Pearce, a collector of stuffed birds, who had a fabulous collection including stuffed eagles and falcons. I thought of a brilliant way of paying Dick back. He had never been abroad before so I asked his wife Jane to sort him out a passport, and I got in touch with Gruppo Cooper in Italy. I told them I would need an assistant to travel with me to help with the eagle for the film, as it would involve flying the eagle backwards and forwards calling him to the fist for a few days when we got to the Alps. I explained it would be too dangerous to give just anyone a glove and let him fly to a stranger's hand. They agreed with me and I revised the fee and they sent me another airline ticket (first class) and booked an extra room in the hotels. I called round to Dick and said the Italian company had agreed to pay me the full fee in pound notes once I arrived at Milan airport with the eagle. I said I wanted the money up front because I had never worked with a foreign company before, they were quite happy to go along with this. I told Dick if he wanted the money for the Tawny Eagle he would have to come to Italy to collect it. I felt this was a great way to repay his wonderful gesture of buying me the eagle, he was getting a free holiday and also getting his money back.

I trained the eagle by taking him to Dunstable Downs where he used to gain a lot of lift by flying off the top of the downs which are 800ft above sea level and it was ideal for getting him to soar. It was about 3000 metres short of the height he was expected to fly for the film work, but it was a start.

In another book I will go into detail of what happened in Italy, as it was a story in itself, but it all worked out in the end and was a huge success. There were lots of mishaps along the way, including Heathrow Airport forgetting to put the eagle on the plane, and us arriving in Italy without him despite the captain announcing, as we flew into Milan airport, "The eagle has landed!" or so he thought.

As well as Dick refusing to eat salmon, caviar and champagne on the flight preferring corn beef sarnies his wife Jane had made him. Also Dick being briefly arrested at the airport by a machine gun wielding, 17 year old, spotty faced, Italian soldier with a nasty Alsatian, for having a strange smelling substance coming out of his Levi jacket pocket. The Alsatian was trained to pick this out, teeth snarling, standing on its back legs trying to go for Dick's throat and had to be restrained by the soldier. Dick was released without charge, thank God! It was funny to watch at the time.

Once Poacher, had eventually arrived on the next available flight from London, we were driven to Milan for a photo shoot at the company headquarters then taken to our hotel rooms for the night.

Having never stayed in such high-class hotels before we thought the alcohol and snacks in the little fridges in our hotel rooms were freebies. We proceeded to empty both of them! What a hangover! What a bill! Luckily it was the Italian TV company that had to pick it up as well as the two hour long international phone calls to our wives! Fair to say we were given a right telling off but they took it all in their stride once the eagle did what I promised them it would do.

The next night we travelled to Turin, but mysteriously the fridges containing the bottles of spirits were missing from our hotel rooms.

Once we arrived at the top of Piccolo Cervino, which we had to reach by cable car, we were treated like celebrities. There was a huge wooden hotel with a fabulous restaurant. When filming started in the morning, a huge crowd gathered to watch the eagle flying. He would fly in large circles gaining height until he was just a spot in the electric- blue, clear sky, not a cloud to be seen for miles. When the camera crew were ready for him to come down I would whistle. One particular morning Poacher was up about 1500-2000 feet circling above us. There was a huge crowd again all pointing to him. I should say at this point they were all wearing skis and snow shoes. The camera crew gave me the nod to call him down. I gave a huge whistle and instead of his normal wings folded stoop he just started coming down slowly in a big circle. All of a sudden, and there's no other way of describing what happened next, he shit! When eagles do that they can slice their mutes, as we call it, about six or seven foot. When that happens at about a 1000 feet in the air it looks like a great big white snake flying across the sky. I knew exactly what the snake was, but the huge crowd had no idea! At this point Poacher was now in a stoop back to my gloved fist with this enormous long white snake directly above the crowd of spectators. I was in hysterics when somebody shouted out in broken German "das is eagle shit!" By the time the crowd realised what was above them it was too late, they tried to move away but were all tripping over each because they were wearing skis and snowshoes. I remember looking at a crowd of about thirty people all in a heap with a load of eagle shit over their bright coloured ski suits. Dick, I and the camera crew had never laughed so much in our lives.

After the film work was completed we were allowed to stay in the Alps to fly the eagle for several days until our flights back. During this time Poacher was allowed to go off on the soar during the day, and forty five minutes later or so I would call him down.

One particular day he was doing just that when he spotted a pair of freshly caught trout lined up by a fisherman's basket at the foot of the Aoster valley, 2000 ft. below where I was flying him. Poacher decided they looked more inviting than the piece of meat I was offering him. The stoop was spectacular but at the time I had no idea where he was off to, or what he was up to. The angler turned out to be a vet, of all things, who upon seeing the eagle devouring one of his freshly caught trout, threw the other trout into the boot of his car. Poacher quickly followed jumping in so as not to lose the other trout. The vet closed the boot, put his fishing rod in the back of the car and drove off to Paola in southern Italy, 800 miles away, with the biggest catch of his life in the boot of the car.

By the time we arrived at the bottom of the valley two hours later with our tracking gear the eagle was nowhere to be seen. I stayed on another week looking for him, to no avail.

We eventually got him back six weeks later after the vet, had contacted DEFRA, UK. Poacher had got a UK cable tie on his leg with its own unique number thus making him traceable. However that was not the end of the story. When he was sent back to me six weeks later, I was arrested at Heathrow airport for trying to smuggle in a Tawny Eagle. The vet had cut the ring off the eagle so he could read the small numbers on the cable tie. I had no means of proving that Poacher was the same eagle I had taken to Italy six weeks earlier. Eventually I convinced the people at animal quarantine he was mine, because I went into the big aviary where they had put him and picked him up without using a glove. They said I was either mad or it was my eagle. An hour later I was on my way home with him. All good fun and ended well.

"Dick if you hadn't made this wonderful gesture then I don't think I would have been in a position today to write this book. Many, many thanks you're more than a great friend."

Dick Smith, with poacher, way up in the Aoster valley near Piccolo Cervino during a break in filming.

I should've called him The Artful Dodger, mugging rabbits, pinching the dog's bones and pilfering trout! He was always up to something.

Later that year I thought I would take him up to Scotland with the Harris Hawks, and pit him against the big boys!

Here are some words by great friend Chris Joinison

The sun was out but its warm rays betrayed the bitter cold winds that would suddenly gust along the channel of the valley and catch us all unawares. The winds being too high again for the cast, so just the female was flown but she had begun to bait at longer and longer slips so things were progressing. She put in a couple of pretty impressive attempts fighting wildly gusting winds proving her growing skills, strength and conviction. We saw wild eagles and peregrines hunting that day, sights which will stay with me all my life. Ian the gamekeeper told us of a valley that ran parallel to the one we were staying in which was more protected from the wind. Judging by the amount of hares that we saw going over the top into it, it would seem they knew of the valleys as well.

So over we went. Climbing, carrying the birds and in heavy clothing was tough work. .

Tom had his Tawny Eagle with him but pushed on as did the rest of us to be rewarded with the world's supply of blue hares racing across the countryside that was opening up below us.

Game on (to coin a phrase I have heard many times whilst out hunting with Home Counties Hawking Club (HCHC). Soon there were three Harris' in the air and chasing, not at all successful but amazing nevertheless. Having recovered my female some distance from the rest of the team and in rapidly deteriorating visibility I saw swept back wings to my left. A double take revealed the Tawny in hot pursuit of a very fast running Hare both disappeared over a small ridge, instantly followed by Tom. Working back across the wind to re-join the others, the weather was rapidly deteriorating and using whistle blasts we closed together slowly.

Once together it soon became apparent that Tom was not with us. We followed the line down the hill in the direction that the Tawny had gone whilst the ever increasing blizzard raged at our backs. Soon it was impossible to see and we beat a hasty retreat to the lower ground in the bottom of the valley. .

We were so high up , the jets were flying below us.

Violent, gusting winds and snow blasting our backs as we made towards the planned rendezvous with the land rover in the hope that Tom had made his way there.

Whilst he was climbing a deer fence Bob's bird baited hard at a close running hare and was free at the very same moment a blast of wind and snow so strong that it knocked every one to the ground and carried the bird with it. We searched in the storm for Bob's bird, desperately trying to stay in touch. After twenty minutes of searching in white-out blizzard conditions the wind suddenly stopped and we were left in silence. Nelly instantly returning to Bob's calls, how she hung on in that wind and blizzard heavens knows but there she was. All the birds now had a mask of ice completely covering their eyes and faces. The problem now was to find Tom for whom concern was growing rapidly, this was remote high moorland in the throes of a hefty storm. He was not at the land rover and after waiting briefly it was decided to return to the castle. Should we not find him back there, then we would alert the mountain rescue and begin a search.

Thankfully Tom was safe and waiting for us at the castle but sadly had not been able to recover his Eagle. Armed with tracking gear and the land rover, Ian's local knowledge and a drag lure we went in search. With growing concern fading light and the intolerance of the resident wild eagle population we searched on twice sighting the Tawny in high cliffs and woodland she could not be tempted down and finally beaten by the light, we were forced to retire for the night. Having yet never spent a night with a bird out the evening was another lesson for me. The whole group shared in Tom's anguish the conversation at supper revolved only around the possibilities and planning for recovery of the eagle the next day. We all went to bed early exhausted from the efforts of the day but also to will the morning to come quickly. The planning paid off, by 10 o'clock the Eagle had landed.

So pleased was the Tawny to see Tom that he gave him a smack in the mouth, splitting his lip in the process. Spirits raised and with a hearty breakfast inside us we set of again for the final days hawking. Bright sunshine and almost perfect winds meant the cast could be flown but the male had some catching up to do. The amount of slips went beyond counting and this time with some considerable success. Tom's unconventional approach to Hare Hawking included the wearing of a white overall and did not require the skills of a bird, it has to be said, the method proved very effective. The week ended with over 26 blue hares being caught."

Chris Joinison

It was around that time that I questioned the time and the effort I had put in with the Tawny Eagle. His temperament was superb but his feet were rather small and although he would catch the hares he very seldom held them long enough for me to arrive and help him. It was time to consider if I was ready for a Golden Eagle. I had spent some time visiting Jim Wood in the early eighties with his Goldie and those memories and his words " You will never do any good till you get a Goldie" were never far from my thoughts. I had done well with several Tawny Eagles and a Steppes Eagle, catching lot's of rabbits but hares were another ball game. The smaller eagles lacked the weight and aggression and the size of their feet were always questionable compared to the big eagles.

When considering this I had no idea how much of an Achilles Heel eagles' feet were to become!

CHAPTER 2

INSPIRATION

alconry has been called the Sport of Kings. The number of monarchs who have felt a special passion for it seems to bear this out. I'm no monarch but I do hold a special passion for eagle falconry. This is where the story about my unique bond with Kaiser really begins, thirty years ago.

My main source of inspiration, to train and hunt a Golden Eagle, came from being invited up to Bonchester Bridge, in the Borders, to spend some time with Jim Wood hunting with his Golden Eagle. This was way back in the early eighties. I had already been a falconer for ten years or more, and at the time I was hunting rabbits with a Tawny Eagle, bred by Philip Dugmore (my mentor). Jim was curious to see it hunting as he had tried with one several years earlier with little success. I took it up to near Askrigg, in the dales, and flew it at rabbits on a day that was so windy aeroplanes were grounded. We caught several bunnies and then I got to go out with Jim and his Goldie. On my way home I knew I wanted a Golden Eagle, it would be only a matter of time. Jim later moved back to Bonchester Bridge and I went up several times to see him hunting with his Goldie. Over the years I lost touch with him but I still treasure the time I spent with him and his eagle. Here are a few words that Jim wrote at the time and I'm quite sure he would be more than happy to see them in print .

Stunning photo of Jim Wood's Golden Eagle and cameraman Hugh Miles, whose award winning documentary, Kingdom of the Ice Bear, was shown on BBC 1

Jim's Goldie was used during the making of the Living Planet featured on BBC 1 In which there was some spectacular filming of his eagle catching blue hares.

"As far back as I can remember birds of prey have held a great fascination for me, and above all, eagles. During the mid-60's I became interested in falconry, to the point that all my spare time was spent either flying a Hawk or Falcon or following someone that was. I have found Falconry to be a most fascinating and accomplished field sport. I have also found Falconers themselves to be, without a doubt, the most caring of conservationists where birds of prey are concerned. Falconry is not a sport one can take lightly, dedication, time, as well as respect for ones tutor must all be taken into account, before one ever thinks about taking falconry up as a hobby.

Falconry is the only field sport that puts the hunted on equal terms with the hunter, allowing the hunted every chance of escape. Unlike a gun or fishing rod, a hawk cannot be put in a cupboard until next required. If for instance one put his Hawk in a mews or shed used for same, for the period of one week after being trained without manning it, i.e. walking with it on the gloved fist for at least an hour every day, or at feeding times just throwing it food, he would soon become wild and alarmed at the trainer's approach and unworkable.

Eagles will not fly well everyday because of their powers of fasting. Even if they are at their true flying weight, they must still be fasted for two or three days, if expected to pursue quarry or at least make a half-hearted attempt.

Another reason is the fact that eagles can hold castings or pellets for as long as four days, before finally ejecting, one must keep a careful check on this. They will also ignore water for long periods, I have only seen my eagle drink water on odd occasions, only on very hot days, as little as three occasions in one year.

Kaiser in Cambridge about to catch another hare in mid-air.

Only eagles can be around for long periods after they have been trained, and still remain workable. All birds used in the practise of Falconry are trained by controlled dieting whereby the trainer decides the bird's intake which is then decided upon by its obedience during training. Eagles are capable of fasting for long periods, which make these birds exceptionally hard to train. They have been recorded to fast for as long as four weeks without experiencing real hardship which must be of great help in the wild when the weather for days on end makes hunting impossible. Before eagles can be trained for hunting all internal fats must first be removed by dieting. If eagles were dieted in the same way as other small birds of prey, by the time the eagle reached its flying weight the hunting season would be over as large eagles must lose pounds rather than ounces.

While flying the bird on low ground a hare was flushed by the beaters and the eagle was slipped. When the eagle came within striking distance of the hare and it was just about to put in for the kill, the hare jumped at least five feet in the air high above the approaching eagle with the result that the hare escaped. I have seen this strange phenomenon on three occasions, once on low ground and twice on high ground. The eagle being unsuccessful on both occasions.

I have been told by other eagle trainers that they have also witnessed the same phenomenon, only one of these other trainers had an eagle that could cope with this strange occurrence by turning upside down, thus seizing the hare with one foot. He told me that she very rarely missed, I would love to have been present, what a sight that must have been!"

Jim with his Goldie

I feel honoured to have read and been inspired by Jim's words. I also feel privileged to have trained an eagle, be it one with a serious handicap, to catch a leaping hare and even more privileged because I captured it on camera, not once but several times.

The picture below is close on thirty years old. I'm holding Jim Wood's Golden Eagle which I believe was one of the last Golden Eagles to be taken under licence in 1980. Jim lived in the old police house at Bonchester Bridge; he is a fascinating guy, who gave up a successful building partnership, in Newcastle with his brother, to go in pursuit of his love for falconry. He managed to get a job as a gamekeeper on the Dalmunzie estate in Glenshee, Perthshire, not an easy thing to do when you fly a Golden Eagle. Many times Jim was shortlisted for a top keeper's job only to lose out once it was found he owned and hunted with a Golden Eagle.

However hearing of his love for falconry the owner of the estate, Mr D Winton, granted Jim permission to fly his Goldie on the estate in his spare time, often coming out to watch him. In the early days when Jim used to fly his eagle on Dalmunzie there were several hundred blue hares on the estate.

I hunted with Kaiser on the estate with Barry Blyther, Roxanne Peggie and Steve the keeper in the years 2009-2012 but the numbers of hares have never been anything like when Jim was there. Gone are the days when five to six hundred blue hares were shot in a day on adjoining estates!

Nearly thirty years on and here I am on the very same estate with Kaiser. It is such a wonderful feeling, you're hunting on the same ground as someone who inspired you and you admired for so long.

"Hope you are well Jim and maybe one day we will catch up again."

Myself, along with great friend Renaat Broos (Ronnie to his friends) and Barry Blyther on the Dalmunzie Estate in GlenShee Perthshire, January 2012.

As said Jim Wood was my main source of inspiration along with a trip to Opočno, in the Czech Republic, in 2002 to see Golden Eagles hunting. The trip was organised by the members of the South East Falconry Group (SEFG) from Tilbury. Let me stop and explain for a minute. Falconry is very big in Europe, especially Hungary, Czech Republic, Slovakia, Austria, and Germany. However to some English falconers, or to me at least, there was some ignorance as to how big and how well it is organised out there.

Opočno is one of the most famous falconry meets in Europe, a must visit. We flew from Stansted early in November 2002. Opočno was celebrating its twenty fifth hunting anniversary and there was around a dozen or so guys from the SEFG plus other falconers from other clubs in the UK. I was thrilled to bits to be going because I knew there would be a large number of hunting Golden Eagles.

When I first started in falconry I very quickly realised that I wanted to have my own Golden Eagle, I didn't appreciate that I would have to wait so long! Anyway, to continue, we were booked into a large hotel in Opočno where many famous falconers, over the years, had stayed when they had come to hunt with their eagles and falcons.

We all registered at the check in and were given various pieces of paperwork, including meal vouchers, passes, and room keys. We had a brief walk round the small town and a few cold beers. We would be joining small hawking parties for the following day's meet. Bob Watkins, Phil Huzzey and I had already decided we were going with one of the groups flying eagles. I think there were at least three or four different eagle parties consisting of between six to ten guys with eagles, mostly Golden Eagles but there was one or two Bonelli's Eagles as well and one flown by Patric Desmet from Belgium which was superb.

Miro Micenko and close friend Lubo Engler, Slovakian eagle falconers, were in the group we chose

It's a great spectacle to see so many eagles together.

14/10/2004

23

During the day Miro let me carry his Goldie and that was it for me, I was addicted! I wanted one of his young Goldies. That day we witnessed many Golden Eagles catching fox, deer and hares. Hares were numerous, most people won't believe that you could get fifty to sixty hares sitting in one field.

Briefly, for those that are unfamiliar with what takes place at the field, I'll describe the event. The eagle falconers form a long line. Depending how many eagles there are determines how far apart from each other the falconers stand. Between any two falconers there are spectators who also form the line, so it's not uncommon to have a line several hundred yards long. When the command is given everybody walks straight out towards the middle of the field.

The next morning, after breakfast, we went out to the weathering at the back of the hotel. It was a spectacular sight, twenty three Golden Eagles all tethered to blocks and bow perches, and some even had umbrellas attached to the sides of their perches.

As the eagles were being loaded into the cars, we hurriedly got into ours. One thing you had to learn very quickly, out there, is that if you hang about they won't wait for you, and you will end up getting lost. Our group consisted of around twelve eagle falconers from Hungary, Austria and Slovakia. I spent most of the day walking along side Miro Micenko, who bred as well as hunted with Golden Eagles. His Goldie was a beautiful big female that regularly caught fox and deer and I believe was, at the time of the meet, seventeen years old and he still bred with her.

The eagle was allowed to rest for a few minutes before being called back to the fist and hooded.

Everybody continued out into the field. Within a few yards another hare got up close by and ran off.

Another eagle was unhooded and released, this time it was a very large female and although she looked to be flying slower than the male once she started moving she quickly gained on the hare and soon closed the gap. In a very few wing beats, her huge talons were striking out at the hare.

Sometimes the hare will stay in its form until it's almost trodden on.

When disturbed, the hare runs to escape capture. The nearest guy, with an eagle to the running hare, shouts out loud and slips his eagle off the glove removing the hood at the same time. Thus, the chase is on. We had only been in the field a few minutes and walked less than ten yards, when a hare was put up; a small male Golden Eagle was unhooded and released in the direction of the hare. Within seconds the eagle was catching up with the hare when all of a sudden the hare turned sharply ninety degrees into the wind, immediately slowing the eagle down and giving the advantage back to the hare. After several attempts at trying to gain back the advantage the eagle gave up.

But in just a blink of an eye the hare leapt a good six foot clear into the air to evade capture.

The eagle landed on the ground and just watched the hare run off to live another day. Female eagles don't have the tight turning circles the males have, however what they do have is enormous feet and huge talons, so when they do catch a hare they very quickly dispatch it themselves. However they come into their own when catching deer.

The photograph from where my logo originated

To watch what happens is spectacular, depending on the experience and age of the eagle and also the experience of the hare. This is why it's called 'The Sport of Kings'. It's a breath-taking sight to watch the eagle closing in on the hare, only for the hare to stop dead in a split second and watch the eagle overshoot making the eagle look clumsy, or at the last second the hare can leap six or seven feet in the air.

During the week-long meeting, including late nights and lots of vodka, a large numbers of deer and fox were caught by the eagles, but not so many hares as they really are very difficult to catch. Throughout our stay we saw many spectacular flights not always ending in a kill, however it was always an astonishing sight. This was my first trip to Opočno although some of the other club members had been before. One of the most hilarious moments of the week came when comedian Phil Huzzey took a call during the day from another SEFG member, who was out with a different eagle group. He asked how our group was getting on? Phil explained that one of the guys with a Golden Eagle has just caught a large wild boar. Before Phil could say that he was only joking the other guy hung up. On our return to the hotel we were greeted by a rush of people with cameras eager to get a photo of the falconer, his eagle and the wild boar it had caught. The story had spread round Opočno like wildfire and poor old Terry Large, who spread the story, got a lot of stick.

Me and 'Uncle Albert'

Miro Micenko

Having spent the week watching the eagles hunting, it didn't take me long to realise that this was now the time to have a word with Miro and put in an order for a male Golden Eagle .

I wanted to come back out in a few years and catch one of these hares, little did I know how much of a challenge this was going to be?

So I ordered a young Golden Eagle from Miro. I wanted a really small male as I didn't fancy carrying an eagle about all day that weighed twelve pounds and besides I only wanted to catch hares. My theory being the smaller the eagle the quicker on the turn!

This was 2002 and the UK licensing laws governing birds of prey, made it impossible to import a Golden Eagle from a non-European Union country.

William Speckaert calling his eagle back to the fist after an unsuccessful slip

If you're into eagles you must at some time go out to the Czech Republic or Slovakia to watch these amazing eagles hunting down hare, deer and fox.

So I would have to wait until Slovakia joined the EU. I should point out there are a number of breeders of Golden Eagles in the UK. All of them successful, many in their own right, and well known eagle falconers.

I wanted a Golden Eagle whose parents were both hunting birds and not one from parents who had been in aviaries all their life and never hunted. That's just my choice! So I got busy with sorting out a new aviary and all the other bits I would need including new a eagle glove and hoods. I also contacted DEFRA in Bristol with regards to the necessary paperwork, DNA certificates, vet certificates, licences and article 10s. In 2004 Slovakia joined the EU, and I was ready! I had kept in touch with Miro Micenko in Slovakia via an interpreter, which I found on the internet at a cost of £30 an hour, "ouch!" This was not the easiest way of completing paperwork, and cost me a couple of hundred pounds in the finish. Eventually It was worth it.

CHAPTER 3

THE EAGLE HAS LANDED

Miro had bred two male Golden Eagles and a female. Clive from the SEFG, in Tilbury and I wanted a small male each. Allan Ames from Eagle Heights was also looking for a male Goldie so Miro managed to get a third male from another eagle breeder in Slovakia. Alan and I arranged that we'd go across to Austria and meet Miro, who was travelling down from Slovakia. We had agreed to meet halfway at a well-known castle in Austria, from which Josef Heibeler ran his falconry displays and breeding programmes. All the paperwork had already been sent from Slovakia to DEFRA in Bristol with the exception of the final DNA sample certificates which were being sent the day before we travelled along with the health certificates which allowed the birds to travel through Europe. We had booked the ferry crossing and everything was arranged for us to meet up the following Saturday lunchtime in Austria.

I planned to travel down Friday evening from Northampton to meet up with Phil Huzzey, a falconer and close friend who lived in London at the time. We had planned to go down to Eagle Heights, a falconry centre in Kent owned by Allan Ames, and put all the eagle boxes in Allan's transit van and drive across to Austria. I spoke to DEFRA at the beginning of the week, and they confirmed that they had been in touch with the Slovakian authorities with regard to A10 and DNA certificates and although they had not received all the paperwork they assured me it would arrive by the end of the week. Therefore I assumed it would be ok to arrange to fetch the eagles at the weekend. I was so excited to be going to fetch my Goldie that I hardly slept a wink all week and by Friday afternoon I was shattered. As I was putting my eagle box in my car Friday afternoon, I got a phone call from DEFRA to say that the Slovakian authorities had faxed all the paperwork for the three young eagles, the DNA certificates, A10 certificates and copies of the health certificates. There was a problem though, as everything had been written in Slovakian! Obvious as they were from Slovakia, but DEFRA informed us we could not go ahead and bring the birds into the UK until all the paper work had been translated! "Bloody hell!" I was livid to say the least, I was an hour away from leaving. I wished I hadn't answered the phone. So that was it for now, frantic phone calls to Slovakia to stop Miro going on a thousand mile trip with the young eagles. Complete utter disappointment.

We now had to wait for DEFRA to do all the translations of the paperwork which wouldn't be ready till the middle of the following week. By Midweek I got the ok from DEFRA but we had a bank holiday coming up the following weekend which meant chaos on the roads and with three young eagles in boxes it would be far too risky getting stuck in traffic jams. Work commitments prevented us going during the week so we arranged everything for two weeks later.

"Have you ever driven on the right?"

Two weeks on and we were all set again until Friday night when Allan Ames telephoned to say he had a large abscess in his mouth and he wasn't in any fit state to drive across Europe in his transit and pick up the birds. "Jesus! Here we go again" I contacted Phil and said we will have to go in my short wheelbase Pajero to pick up the eagles. My immediate concern was if we would be able to get three big eagle boxes in the car? But we managed. So Phil and I set off for Dover to catch the midnight ferry. I had a close friend print me out a route finder at the last minute. We were sitting on the ferry having a cuppa when Phil asked "Have you ever driven on the right?" Strange he should ask that as I was just about to ask him the same! When I told him that I hadn't, he told me "Don't muck about, I'm serious!" I had never driven in Europe. Luckily Phil had (he forgot to tell me it was a motorbike he had ridden) but wasn't happy with the prospect of having to drive close on two thousand miles. I said "Don't worry I'll keep you awake!"

We crossed to Calais by ferry; our journey was to take us through France, Holland, Belgium and across Germany to the Austrian border. We headed through France, using my last minute route finder. After about seven hours of driving Phil said we should be coming up to Munich soon, but after another two hours there was no sign of Munich!

My friend had spelt it wrong on the route finder and we'd driven 250 miles in the wrong direction. Need to blame Jane Smith for that one, who now runs one of the biggest lorry driving agencies in the country; no wonder there's traffic jams every bank holiday! This was a nightmare, but eventually we found our way to Rosenberg Castle where we were to meet up with the guys from Slovakia.

We had a good look round the castle, and met some of the falconers at the centre while we waited for Miro to arrive. A short while later Miro and Lubo Engler appeared with the eagles. I struggled to contain my excitement, there were three big boxes with three young eagles in them and I got first pick.

Miro with Kaiser's mum

We got them out one at a time to check everything was ok, they were all perfect but I had no idea which one to have, so I asked Miro to pick one but it must be one that he'd bred. He pointed to the last eagle we had just looked at and told me to have this one it will be fine. Ok, that will do, so we sorted out the paperwork and handed over the Euros. In 2004 the eagles cost 2,200 Euros which was a good price. I think it was around £1860. Golden eagles in the UK were around £3000, but as said earlier I wanted one whose parents were still hunting. A couple of handshakes later and we were on our way back. We stopped for a cuppa and a bite to eat in Germany and Phil asked what I was going to call my eagle? I said that I had no idea, but to give me a minute. We were now having a sandwich in Germany and as I was born in Berlin I thought it had to be a German name. Adolph didn't sound too good, my middle name is Hans and I thought about that for a minute or two then came up with "THE KAISER" or "Kaiser" for short. Just at that moment I got stung on my ear by a wasp, I've never been stung before. Phil couldn't stop laughing, must be an omen or something! Within half an hour my ear was like a cauliflower and stung like hell, the Germans have big wasps! I reckon it must have been a hornet. Phil reckoned it was a doodle bug! After that, apart from a brief spell with Phil falling asleep at the wheel, we made it back safely to the UK.

First stop Eagle Heights to give Allan his Goldie. I took one look at Allan's face, it was all swollen from his abscess and he struggled to talk, but it didn't stop him taking the 'Mick' out of my cauliflower ear! Suddenly, I was stung again, on my other ear! This was just outrageous, what on earth is going on? Never in my life have I been stung and in less than twelve hours I had been stung on both ears. Phil was in hysterics, I wasn't amused. Anyway we set off back to Phil's where Clive met us and he took the other eagle, and I duly set off home with Kaiser in the back, a round trip of around eighteen hundred miles in forty eight hours, but now I was home.

"Just at that moment I got stung on my ear by a wasp, ..."

Miro breeds his Golden Eagles by artificial insemination, the semen coming from a male Golden Eagle and then kept frozen until required. Kaiser has only ever seen his mum; the term we use for this in falconry is 'social imprint.' From the moment he was hatched he was reared by his mother in an aviary with his brother and sister. Miro, who breeds the eagles, plays the role of the father and assists the mother feeding and bringing up the chicks. In Slovakia it's called 'dual imprinting' as opposed to 'imprinting.' Thus the eagle is bought up with both eagle and human, not just humans, as this is what is thought to make them aggressive.

Kaiser looking good just a week or so after bringing him in from Slovakia.

Kaiser's mum is flown every season by Miro so is well bonded to Miro and therefore he is accepted in the aviary when the breeding season comes round. To all intent and purpose Kaiser thinks he's a human being. This makes for a really good hunting bird as he likes human company. Not all eagles are bought up in this way, there are pros and cons, but certainly out in Eastern Europe there are lots more socially imprinted eagles than total parent reared eagles (those who have no contact with humans while growing up).

Photo illustrates Kaiser's set up; a wire trace runs along the ground from inside his aviary and up to the top of the garden. Every morning I opened the sliding door on the aviary and he would fly up and down all day. Every night he would fly back inside the aviary on his own, and when I came home from work I just closed the sliding door.

02/10/2004

He settled in very quickly, In all the years I kept and trained other eagles, I knew he was going to be special, nothing seemed to phase him. He was a pleasure to work with..

Training Kaiser started the minute I fetched him from Slovakia, spending time with him, picking him up, carrying him on the fist, it is all part of training, much the same as with any other bird of prey used for falconry. So for the first month that's practically all I did with him, picking him up from his aviary every morning putting him on his large block, and bow perch in the garden and putting out a fresh bath every day. I always felt it important to give Kaiser a choice of block or bow.

Eagles love to bath and Kaiser was no exception, sometimes he would jump in the bath while I was still filling it. As soon as I left him alone he would start singing his head off, "chupping" loudly to let the other birds know that he was having a bath.

It's important to bond with your eagle while it's still growing, as it allows the bird to get used to you and to give it confidence.

At that time, he was not flying at all but he would hold onto his perch by his feet and flap his wings furiously, exercising. I would carry Kaiser around for hours in the garden, sitting on the fist, getting him used to me and his surroundings. From then on I would walk round the local fields getting him used to cattle and dog walkers and anybody that stopped and wanted to have a look at him.

When a young eagle is fully grown we call it "hard penned." This is when the eagle's feathers are fully matured; it means the eagle is ready for training. Once he was hard penned we could move onto stage two of training. He was already comfortable with eating off the fist but now I needed to start making him jump to the fist. With an eagle that has never flown before that's quite a big step and to get it to jump just a few feet has to be done carefully.

Roland Richardson with his Steppes Eagle on the weighing scales. He is wearing one of my leather falconry bags.

I used to weigh Kaiser every day and at the time of picking him up from Slovakia he was still growing and his weight was gaining daily. In the initial stages an eagle can eat as much as it wants, but eventually there is a need to remove some of the puppy fat for training to progress further. The food intake is reduced and the response of the eagle is dependent on the experience of the trainer. I had already been a falconer for some twenty years having flown several African Tawny Eagles and Russian Steppes Eagles for display and hunting, so I was used to handling such a large bird. Within a matter of days I had got him to sit on a set of converted weighing scales, the type you would see in the grocer's shop for weighing up to 14lbs of spuds. We converted them by putting a perch on the top and the eagle quickly learns to like the perch and weighing is easy.

Kaiser jumping to the fist for the very first time. My ex-wife, Lynda, had to stand patiently for nearly half an hour to get this photo.

35

I picked Kaiser up when he was around twelve or thirteen weeks old and he still had several weeks to go before being ready to be trained for hunting. But he was ready to have some leather jesses fitted to his legs so he could be tethered, thus enabling him to sit out in the garden and observe what was to become routine for him.

Eagles and most falconry birds of prey are now, what's called "free lofted." This loosely means they are kept in an aviary once trained, but are taken out during the day to sit on a block or perch to 'weather.'

"Wish I had learnt that with Lynda!"

Most eagles, during the hunting season, are weighed on a daily basis as this is an excellent indicator to the bird's health and condition. If a bird starts to lose weight you won't notice it unless you regularly weigh them and in order to fly them successfully they need to be kept at a given weight depending on their gender and size. Kaiser has a flying weight of around six and a half pounds. Four ounces either side of that and he's fine. If his weight goes above six and three quarters he loses interest in chasing hares and equally if his weight falls below six and a quarter pounds he doesn't have enough energy to sustain long flights to chase the hares.

Every eagle is different in its flying weight; some of the big female Golden Eagles have a flying weight of twelve to thirteen pounds. It also depends on the weather, in the cold they will eat more than if it's hot; but if your eagle is doing a lot of flying during training it will require more than an eagle that doesn't do as much training.

'Horse's for courses!' Here the common sense rule applies, they need to be kept a bit like an athlete who doesn't want to carry any more weight than he needs but he must also be able to maintain enough energy to see him through his race.

Kaiser always gets well fed at the end of the day and he is always rewarded during the day if he catches anything. To give you a general idea, he eats roughly four to six ounces of good quality food a day. If it's really cold he might need six to eight ounces, again depending on how much work he is doing. Food mainly consists of what he catches i.e. hares.

While I was in Slovakia for 3 months (2011) hares were difficult to come by but deer was readily available. My friend Lubo Engler used to be called out by the police to pick up road casualty deer, which were plentiful. Sometimes I would treat him to good quality rump steak, a round trip of fifty miles to get him some, he ate better than I did. You must never rely on your scales alone there is no substitute for knowing the behaviour patterns of your eagle. After having Kaiser for eight years I can tell just by looking at him how well he is and what mood he is in. Wish I had learnt that with Lynda!

Back to training Kaiser, reducing his weight is by far the most important part of training. It's so easy for the inexperienced falconer to rush this by starving an eagle and then you have one extremely dangerous eagle on your hands. Let me say, here and now, very rarely does somebody ever sell a good car, or horse, or eagle, and many a good eagle has been ruined by trying to starve it into submission. Once you starve your eagle it will become extremely aggressive whenever it sees food and probably for the rest of its life it will be unpredictable and dangerous. I know of numerous occasions where this has been done. People own eagles who shouldn't, because they don't have the basic knowledge and understanding of what they are doing or how an eagle behaves.

One golden rule I adopt when flying Kaiser is, I never ever, ever allow him to fly off the fist and look for hares on his own. He is only ever slipped off the fist when I see the hare. First I'm a sportsman, I'm not interested in numbers of hares Kaiser catches and I don't care if he catches one in a season or a hundred.

Some people think they're better falconers because their bird has caught hundreds. In thirty years of falconry I've caught more than I care to count.

I've watched Kaiser chase hares and some days I'm willing the hare to escape because just watching him is breath-taking, it's the thrill of the chase that appeals to me. Hopefully you will understand what I mean when you see some of my photographs of birds of prey hunting.

I control what he chases, and if a hare gets up too close to me I don't take Kaisers hood off until I think there's a good fifty per cent chance that the hare can get away.

This is extreme hawking, the hunter and the hunted on equal terms, The other reason that I choose to hunt off the fist as opposed to putting the eagle up a tree or allowing him to fly off hunting on his own, is that eagles don't know the difference between a hare and a small dog running along the side of a field.

Some might say that if you're hunting on private land with permission, the dog shouldn't have been there, but that's not the point. All eagle falconers have a huge responsibility to take care of the sport. We are self-governing, and although it's not that difficult to train an eagle to hunt, that's only a small part of eagle falconry. There is so much more to consider. It's also about keeping the sport of falconry alive, as eagle falconers attract more attention and the eyes of the world are watching. I'm extremely passionate about what I do, and I'm also very much aware how many other people are just as passionate.

Several guys in Slovakia hunt their eagles out of trees especially, in the forests when they are hunting deer. Martin Hollinshead also hunted this way in Austria. Eagles will follow on and it's also a great way of keeping the eagle fit. However the drawback to this is that you can only fly one eagle at a time in this way, and if not very careful they can quickly learn to self-hunt. Glyn Thompson has trained Otto, his eagle, to follow on in the woods, but Glyn only does it for about five percent of his overall flying time.

Back to getting some weight off Kaiser, there are several ways of doing this. One way, without him knowing, is to feed him washed rabbit meat with plenty of rabbit fur still left on. This gives him the same amount of bulk food so he still has a crop full but he won't put weight on. Washed rabbit meat is rabbit that has been allowed to soak, reducing the blood in the meat, giving him less protein.

This is a slow process that can take up to six weeks or more depending on how much the eagle weighs at the start of training. I once read that eagles can have almost a third of their bodyweight taken off, this is just guide but it's not far out. Kaiser has a top weight of around just over nine pounds and flies at about six. I don't generally allow his weight to get up to nine pounds as it can take a long time to get him fit and his weight down. Kaiser's weight is allowed to go up during the summer when he's not being hunted, as he will be moulting and growing new feathers.

Eagles take about six weeks to grow new primary and tail feathers. For Kaiser to lose a couple of pounds, when at most he will only lose an ounce a day, takes a long time, especially as he still needs to be fed during this time as well. A point of interest for people who are not falconers, eagles in the wild will catch a hare and gorge themselves to the point where their stomach and crop will be so full of food that they can last up to seven or eight days without hunting again, depending on the time of year. During the late seventies there was a programme called Survival. One episode was about a pair of Golden Eagles breeding in the Cairngorms in Scotland. The female eagle was covering the eggs and the male was sitting on a nearby crag. The film crew had to pack up and leave because the weather was so bad. They put a time-lapse camera on the male Golden Eagle and for the next twenty two days the eagle didn't move. On the twenty third day he was seen to return to the crag with a freshly caught blue hare which he shared with the female. I had a Russian Steppes Eagle that went thirty two days without food. After the thirty second day it flew to my fist, ate half the chick and then didn't want to fly another ten yards for the other piece of food. It spent the rest of the day preening its feathers and bathing.

"For Kaiser to lose a couple of pounds, when at most he will only lose an ounce a day, takes a long time, especially as he still needs to be fed during this time as well."

It was a big female with a top weight of eleven and a half pounds and eventually it did catch a few rabbits, but that was with almost four and a half pounds of fat taken off. For falconry purposes we couldn't hunt with a bird that was full of food in that way so we give the bird enough food to last him the day, which ensures the next day he will still be hungry. However you can't fly them on an empty stomach for too long so it's a finely tuned balance. Because of their ability to fast, eagles never perform well if flown every day like Harris Hawks. If Kaiser gets fed every day he gets too comfortable, and only half heartedly chases hares to keep me happy! So I keep him on his toes during the hunting season trying to imitate how he would get fed if he was wild. Sunday night, at the end of a weekends hunting, I give him enough food to last him for the next four days all in one go then I give him nothing for the next three days, that way by the Saturday morning he is ready to go hunting and still at his best flying weight.

CHAPTER 4

DISASTER

K aiser's weight was coming down nicely and he was jumping to the fist. I had just started putting him on a light training line called a 'creance' (lightweight nylon cord wrapped round a wooden handle around 50 metres long), and he would fly to my gloved fist for a small piece of meat held in my hand.

He was flying around 20 feet half a dozen times a day; I was planning to take him into the field at the top of the garden by the end of the week so I could get him to fly further distances on the training line. It was now October, I was just putting Kaiser in his aviary for the night and was checking his feet as I did two or three times a week. It's very easy for a young eagle to puncture its own feet with its talons while being trained as it's constantly opening and closing its feet whilst flying to the fist. I noticed a very tiny puncture wound on the side of his big toe near the end by the talon. It was a very tiny wound, at the time I thought it had been possibly caused by a staple sticking out of the aviary as all the netting was new and secured by staples. I thought I would keep an eye on it, as it really was tiny and it couldn't have been more than a couple of days old.

By the end of the week I felt Kaiser's toe and it appeared to be warm although there was no swelling and the tiny pin prick hadn't got any worse. I was concerned though, that a warm toe was not a good sign. I now faced a dilemma.

I was flying on the following Tuesday to be a spectator at an eagle meet in Sečovce, in Slovakia, with the guys from the SEFG and was unsure if I should leave Kaiser. My concern was that I wouldn't be able to keep an eye on his toe, although my ex-wife was very good at handling my birds including Kaiser. She had been an accomplished falconer in her own right many years ago, hunting with a female Sparrow Hawk for several seasons, but gave it up when our son was born. I knew that whilst I was away she would keep me informed. However because Kaiser was still growing I felt his immune system was probably not fully developed and therefore I would be happier if he had a shot of antibiotics in him. I hadn't used a vet for several years so I rang close friend Mike Hewlet for advice. He is a well-known falconer who runs a private centre, Icarus falconry, for breeding and running falconry experience days, just on the outskirts of Northampton.

11/10/2004

14/10/2004

Mike suggested a vet I had used two years previously, Stewart, who had returned to the area from Yorkshire. Stewart, was now treating birds of prey again. So I rang him and arranged to see him that afternoon. I put Kaiser in his box and took him over.

Stewart thought it was a blackthorn wound despite the fact that Kaiser hadn't been out of the garden. He gave him a seven day course of Marbocyl, explaining it was a really good broad-spectrum antibiotic and although it wasn't licenced as yet for birds of prey, it was well used by vets across the country for this purpose. Most veterinary antibiotics are designed for horses, cats and dogs, but are used on other animals. So Kaiser was put on a seven day course of Marbocyl. I told Stewart I was flying out to Slovakia the next day for five days and if there was a problem could my ex-wife, Lynda, bring him back? He said that wouldn't be a problem but as the antibiotics were a seven day course I would be back by then and in any event they should do the trick.

14/10/2004

Adrian Frost with Bob Watkins

I asked Stewart if Kaiser should have a swab taken and he said that it wasn't necessary. 'Always insist on a swab!'

I took him back home and as I was leaving for Slovakia in the morning gave Lynda instructions to ensure he got his antibiotics, something she has done many times over the last twenty years or so, with other birds I had kept. I would be back on the Sunday afternoon and she would keep me informed if there was a further problem. While I was away Lynda telephoned me, on the Friday afternoon, to say Kaiser's toe had begun to swell and discolour. She had telephoned Stewart explaining that she wanted him seen, but he told her it wasn't necessary because Kaiser was still on his course of antibiotics and any swelling was normal. I felt helpless as there was nothing I could do other than wait till I got back from Slovakia.

I got back home mid-morning on the Sunday and was horrified when I saw Kaiser's toe. It looked absolutely dreadful and I immediately feared the worse.

To me it looked like it was broken at the end, the toe was severely swollen and twisted I rang the vets immediately and spoke to Tom the assistant vet. I explained how bad Kaiser's toe was looking and that I wanted him seen straight away. He said Stewart wouldn't be in till the next day and told me to bring him over first thing in the morning. I insisted that he needed to be seen immediately and I was bringing him straight over and he should get in touch with Stewart right away.

Tom met us on arrival and I showed him Kaiser's toe. He was concerned how serious it looked. He said to leave Kaiser with him and he would get Stewart to ring me as soon as he had looked at it, I suggested he needed an urgent x-ray.

Tom rang me later on in the afternoon to say Stewart would look at the bird first thing Monday morning and he was booked in for an x-ray at eleven and they would ring me as soon as they had the results.

Monday mid-day I telephoned the vets and was upset to be notified that Kaiser still hadn't been x-rayed, so I told them I would be over straight away. On arrival I was told that Kaiser had just been x-rayed and no bones were broken. They had taken a swab and sent it off. Something I had asked for a week previously. I explained that I wasn't at all happy with the treatment that they had given to Kaiser as he wasn't responding, and explained that I wanted an immediate referral to an expert vet and would they please contact Neil Forbes from GT.Western Referrals and get me booked in as soon as possible. I said that I thought his toe had gangrene and there was a real possibility that Kaiser would lose it. I put Kaiser in the car and whilst driving home Tom the assistant vet rang to say he had got me booked in to Neil Forbes in Swindon first thing the next morning. I advised them they would be hearing from my solicitor in due course!

19/10/2004

" I wanted an immediate referral to an expert vet …"

GREAT WESTERN EXOTICS

Our team is led by Neil Forbes DipECZM (avian) FRCVS. Neil is an RCVS and European Recognized Specialist in Avian Medicine. Neil graduated from the Royal Veterinary College in 1983 with a 1st Class Honors degree. He gained his RCVS Specialist status in 1992 and his FRCVS by examination in Exotic Bird Medicine in 1996. He gained his European Diploma (European Recognized Specialist) in 1997.

Great Western Exotics unit 10 Berkshire House, county Business Park, Swindon SN1 2NR Tel: 01793 603 802   Fax: 01793 603 801
Email: swindonreferralsexotics@vets-now.com

I was dreadfully upset that Kaiser might lose his big toe and that would, effectively, be the end of a ten year dream. Without his big toe he wouldn't survive in the wild, and as a hunting bird, in captivity, he would be all but useless. I was at Great Western Exotics for 9 am the following day to be met by Neil Forbes, who immediately looked at Kaiser's toe, and said it didn't look good but to get him upstairs and see what could be done.

Neil wanted to know what treatment Kaiser had been given, as he had not been told too much by the other practice that was treating him. I explained that he was on a seven day course of Marbocyl which had just finished, but they had only just taken a swab test.

Neil came back down about an hour later and said Kaiser's toe was all but hanging off and it was full of gangrene and would be far too dangerous to be left on, and very sadly he had no alternative but to remove his big toe.

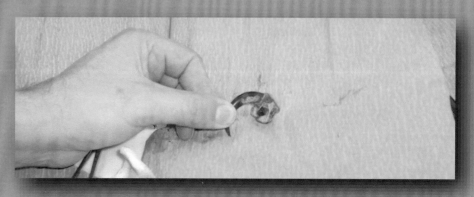

44

I was devastated, I had waited almost twenty years to own a Golden Eagle, then a further wait for Slovakia to be an EEC member. To finally get one and find he has to have his main hunting talon and toe removed, was just awful. I hadn't even flown him free up to this point.

I felt absolutely gutted. Neil said that it wasn't the end of his problems. We still didn't know why he hadn't responded to the antibiotics and the likely hood was, the infection was still in his blood stream. It needed to be identified, before it went into the rest of his body and kill him. Neil had already taken swabs and started him on several other antibiotics, but was perplexed as to why he wasn't responding to Marbocyl which should have done the job.

Once Kaiser had come round from his operation he was kept at Neil's for a few days to recover and to wait for the results of swab test. Within a couple of days Neil came back to me with the results of the swabs and said Kaiser had a bug called Morganella which should have been treated successfully with the Marbocyl the other vet had prescribed.

I knew my ex-wife, Lynda, had been giving Kaiser the tablets while I was away so I was at a loss as to why he hadn't responded. Neil said he was now concerned because the bug Morganella had now mutated into a really nasty bug, Morganella Morganii, and they were trying to find a suitable antibiotic to treat Kaiser but it wasn't easy because the bug had become immune to all the known antibiotics that vets used. In the mean time I went down to Neil's and picked Kaiser up. He still had lots of stitches, and antibiotic beads had been placed inside his toe or what was left of his toe. I still had to take him back to Neil's every four days to have his dressing changed and to have more swab tests.

I was having to give Kaiser two injections in his chest and two in his legs twice a day.

Trying to cast a Golden Eagle and inject it at the same time was not easy, even with his hood on he struggled, I can't blame him! My concern was that he would come to resent me doing this to him, so I would get Lynda to hold Kaiser after I had injected him, then when she took his hood off he only saw her.

21/10/2004

Here is Lynda, holding Kaiser while I gave him his injections.

Not many women could do this as he was very strong with his grip. She was also allergic to penicillin. One day she opened one of the aviary doors where my Steppe's Eagle, Gunga Din, was waiting to ambush her. As she threw a dead rabbit in the aviary the Steppe's Eagle seized her arm. She was terribly brave she was on her own and it took some getting off. Because she was allergic to penicillin it took a long time to heal.

I had been going back and forth to Neil's for about three weeks, a round trip of some 150 miles twice a week. Neil was getting concerned that the antibiotics we were using weren't killing off the infection and at any time it could flare up and go into the rest of Kaiser's body.

At that moment it was being contained in what small piece of toe he had left. We had no help from the previous vets as they claimed they also sent off a swab, and claimed the results had come back and there was no infection. (Statement later withdrawn) I was sitting at home when I suddenly had a brainwave. I went straight into Kaiser's veterinary medicine box, and looked up the manufacturers of Marbocyl. They were based in Oxfordshire. I spoke to one of their employees who said that Marbocyl wasn't licenced for birds of prey, but they accepted it was widely used to treat them. I gave them the weight of Kaiser and asked them if they could provide me with a guide as to how much per kilo the dose rate should be in milligrams. To my astonishment they came back to me and said Kaiser would need approximately SEVENTY milligrams per day of Marbocyl. I had looked on the empty box from the vets and he had been prescribed seven point five milligrams per day! (See photos)

I told the manufacturers this and they said it sounded like the vet had used the dose rate recommended for cats and dogs! Birds of prey need considerable more. I got straight on to Neil Forbes at Great Western Referrals. I told him what the manufactures of Marbocyl had said, and also that I would email a photo of the dose rate from the empty box of Marbocyl. No wonder Kaiser hadn't responded!

Kaiser was massively under dosed. The bug had built up immunity, as it had been fed small amounts of Marbocyl. Here was all the evidence I needed for my solicitor to bring a case against the first vets for negligence. Sadly that wasn't helping Kaiser, although we now know why he didn't respond. At that moment in time we were using all sorts of antibiotics to try and kill this bug that had mutated to become a very serious infection. With the results of the last grown set of cultures Neil rang with bad news. The ministry that were doing the tests on the bug had said if we couldn't kill the bug within the next ten days, we would have to put Kaiser down, because the bug keeps mutating and it's extremely dangerous. I will always remember Neil saying to me if we have to put him down then we will have to do it in the car park, because if this bug gets into his practise it could ruin him.

Again I was devastated it had been a month since Kaiser had his toe removed, and I hoped we would be winning. One of Neil's assistants came from Germany and she had been back there for the weekend and returned with new antibiotics. Armed with these and knowing why Marbocyl hadn't worked, Kaiser was placed on a seven day course of the new antibiotics. This really was his last chance! I waited for the results of the last culture not knowing if Kaiser had to be put down or if the antibiotics had killed the bug. Within a couple of days Neil's phone number lit up on my mobile phone while I was driving home. I thought "God" I really don't want to answer this. Neil's first words were, "Great news Tom we have it under control Kaiser will be ok." Unbelievable! I didn't really know what to say. I was just so relieved. That was a defining moment. I decided I wasn't going to confine Kaiser to a life in an aviary or use him just for displays, I was going ahead with my goal to train a Golden Eagle to catch a Slovakian hare and I was still going to do it with Kaiser.

I didn't care how long it would take me, or that it was an almost impossible task. Kaiser had been through so much, having to have the injections in his chest and legs every day for a couple of months, he deserved the chance.

My veterinary fees for Kaiser came to just over £3500, more money than I paid for Kaiser himself. I took legal action against the first veterinary practice for negligence and thankfully they settled out of court although until this day they've never admitted liability.

"Great news Tom, we have it under control Kaiser will be ok."

Yet again he just seemed to take everything in his stride.

It was near the end of November and I thought I would not try any hunting with Kaiser till the following year. For now I decided to get my camera equipment out and go and take some photos of 'Essex boys' as I call them, SEFG members, hunting with their falcons and hawks. I felt it was still important to take Kaiser with me and carry him on the fist, at the club meets, and summer shows, so he could learn what was going on.

I spent the hunting season with just my camera equipment going to club meets, here and back out in the Czech Republic. I hadn't given up with Kaiser but he had been through a lot, so I took things slowly with him. He was flying quite well in the fields at the back of the garden but the end of the toe that was removed was very tender and soft, it needed time to harden up and I had to cover his blocks and bow perches with silicon to stop the end of his toe becoming sore.

Many years ago I started doing one day courses teaching falconry. The guys in the photo, left, ended up being my best friends. They came on the courses and worked for me during the summer, flying falcons at my displays. Needless to say they have learnt so much more on their own since, and are now teaching others. Well done boys! I'm proud how well you have both done, both running their own falconry centres. Mike at Holdenby in Northamptonshire and Richard at Twin Lakes in Melton Mowbray.

I have been a member of The South East Falconry Group, although I always refer to them on Facebook as Essex Boys, for more years than I care to remember. The club has lots of hunting ground in the Cambridgeshire and the Newmarket area which we use in the winter months, and in the summer give falconry demonstrations at game and country fairs.

Another former student from my one day courses. Anne Becket Bradshaw, with Gunga Din my Steppes Eagle, at an international field meeting in Malham Yorkshire. Anne later went on to be SEFG Club Secretary for a number of years and an accomplished falconer in her own right, hunting with Harris Hawks and Lanner Falcons.

49

Bob Watkins, the land controller for the club, has had some great success hunting both brown and blue hares with his Harris Hawks. So have club members Kevin Parker, Ian Golding and Ian Starling all excellent falconers who own all the Harris Hawkes that are photographed in this book except one. A superb photo of mine of a Harris Hawk catching a blue hare in Scotland, which belonged to Chris Joinison, a very close friend. The photos of Goshawks, in this book, belong to either Neil Sparkes, Robin Moore or Bill Buck all SEFG members. There are one or two photos of Bonelli's Eagles owned by Bill Buck, Mark Dunn or Mike Hewlett. The photos of the Redtail belong to Wayne Beattie. During publishing I may well get some of the photos confused with whose birds belong to whom, but we are all good friends and no offence intended. Although I took the photos, I just want to say that I'm forever grateful to all you guys for letting me use them in the book.

Who ate all me pies?

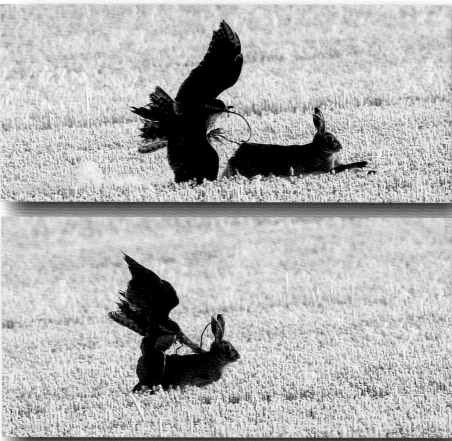

Too many names to mention, but you all know who you are. Six eagles in all, with Gary, Jamil, Richard, Mike, Roland, and myself with Kaiser.

I also spent some time with the newly formed Northampton Raptor Club. We had a really good field meet at my old stomping ground in Malham taking over the infamous Bunk Barn for a number of days. I think there were at least six eagles at the meet, sadly the land had been over hunted and rabbits were scarce but none-the-less good times were had by all. Especially when Jamil was caught poaching on adjoining land and started speaking in Punjabi, we nearly all got shot!

"I can't believe he got that spot he was still having his breakfast when I left."

Another early bird getting a good spot, N R C Chairman, Glynne Malkin.

Hurry up, I need the loo as well!

CHAPTER 5

STOKE MANDERVILLE

It was Christmas day 2004. Every Christmas day for the past five years or so, and this year was no different, I had played golf. Just 9 holes with my son, Fraser, on Collingtree Park golf course. First thing Christmas morning we would sneak out knowing everybody would be at home opening presents, we'd get a freebie! On the way home we would have a game of pool in the local pub and a few beers, before making our way back for Christmas dinner.

My son is an excellent golfer, playing off plus two and holding numerous county records, making the final qualification at the British Open Golf Championship at St Andrews in 2007.

I use to play off six but that's light years away from plus two. However I did win the Buckinghamshire Senior Men's Open in 2008. Between us we have had five holes in one, in official club and county competitions and matches. I had two and my son had three including his home club's short par four, of some 285 yard. Not sure if it's a record, five holes in one for father and son, but something I'm extremely proud of.

I would get my own back on the pool table I almost turned professional pool player back in the seventies. I did my fair share of hustling, and was called out of retirement in the mid-nineties to captain a Northampton team along with close friends Adrian Frost and John Sullivan. Needless to say we won the league hands down only losing one game in sixteen matches. I can still play a mean game or two. Good friend and Falconer Allan Van Vynck can also play a mean game, which reminds me Allan; Keith Sweetman still owes us fifty quid for the match we played at his barbeque. I was feeling pretty pleased with myself by the time I got home, apart from being a little bit the worse for wear.

"Bang! In a split second …"

I'd won several games of pool and downed quite a few bottles of Budweiser, my prize for beating my son. It was at this point Fraser's mum said that she'd be serving up dinner in ten minutes. Fraser asked if we could take some pictures of Kaiser for his friends, I agreed but said to do it before dinner as I wanted another drink after lunch! So Fraser got his camera and I got a couple of pieces of quail for Kaiser to eat.

Kaiser was sitting on his large block in the garden so I bent down and got him to jump to my fist while my son was taking his pictures. All was going well. Kaiser had just eaten a piece of quail meat when I started to stand up, when the other piece of meat that I had in my pocket fell out and dropped to the floor. It's at this point where sheer stupidity kicks in, too many beers! I knew the very second I attempted to pick up the piece of meat that I couldn't get to it before Kaiser did. My brain was telling me don't do that, but the beer was saying go on Tommy pick it up!

Bang! In a split second Kaiser had hit my un-gloved hand with his good foot, just my luck, and I could see as well as feel the damage! He had gone clean through my hand and my index finger, what the heck do I do now? He was gripping really tightly, the piece of meat was wedged under my hand and he was trying to eat it. At the same time, I was trying to keep as still as I could. The pain was unbearable, he had gone through the bone in my hand and I was bleeding quite badly. Kaiser was trying to use both feet on me. I looked up and my son was laughing his head off, not realising how much trouble I was in! Fraser's mum had just shouted through the door "Dinner's ready." I thought that's all I wanted to hear she's going to kill me if we miss dinner!

My son asked if there was anything he could do! I told him to quickly get the hosepipe, turn it on and spray Kaiser on his back. I've seen this work once before when a zoo keeper had been attacked by a black panther which had grabbed the guy on the back of the neck, I was standing six foot away at the time it was not a pretty site. Instantly Kaiser let me go, thank God it worked.

I was in extreme agony, but I had to hide it from my ex-wife. I managed to grab an old piece of rag from the shed and wrap it round my hand intending to have a proper look at the damage after I'd had my turkey and Christmas pudding. I sneaked in, sat down and hid my hand under the table while Lynda served up the dinner. My son kept grinning at me and I tried not to attract attention. My ex suddenly asked why I was only using one hand to eat, at this point my son burst out laughing explaining that Kaiser had nailed me in the hand.

Lynda asked to see, here we go more pain! I looked at the floor and there was blood everywhere, but when I looked at my hand I nearly fainted it was a real mess of torn flesh with a big hole in the middle. She told me to go to hospital and fast. I said I was just going to finish my turkey and brussel sprouts. So I wolfed my dinner down and left my son to devour the lovely mince pies and sherry trifle and off I shot to the hospital, I had a Range Rover automatic so I managed to drive one-handed.

On arrival at A&E I was seen quickly. Christmas day lunchtime it was empty apart from an idiot that had been nailed by a Golden Eagle! The doctor realised the tendons had been damaged and I needed to be sent elsewhere for urgent, specialist attention. I refused the ambulance, stating that I had a friend in the car who could drive me so he rang Stoke Mandeville Hospital to inform them I would be coming over. I shot home to tell them what had happened and to stuff a dozen mince pies in a bag, ten of which I ate on the way. An hour later I arrived at Stoke Mandeville feeling pleased that I had driven, one handed, all the way on my own!

By the time I got there news had travelled fast and I had become a celebrity. The doctors said they'd never had anyone who'd been attacked by a Golden Eagle before, let alone on Christmas day. They whipped me into the operating room to have a closer look at my hand under a huge big spotlight. There must have been a dozen of them all poking about.

The doctor in charge said it looks like there's a fair bit of tendon damage and a piece of bone missing from your index finger so this is going to take a couple of hours to clean up. We will have to knock you out for an hour or two. "Have you had anything to eat?" "Ha ha!" I laughed out loud, and told them that in the last two hours I'd eaten a full Christmas dinner and in the last three quarters of an hour ten lovely mince pies, why? "Oh dear!" the doctor said, we can't anesthetise you. I said "Don't worry I'll come back tomorrow, Benny Hill's on tonight and I don't really want to miss that." At that he told me I was going nowhere till it was sorted out, they would just have to do it with local anaesthetic. Not realising what this entailed I was feeling good that I wasn't being put under. That soon changed during next two and a half hours as I was given fourteen injections in my hand plus I was laying on the table with a mass of spotlights on my face with a big mirror above me. I could see every little detail of what they were doing to me and I could still feel pain, it was not good!

Eventually they were finished and the doctor said he'd get me booked into a bed for a couple of days and would come and see how my finger is behaving. "A BED!! Your joking I can't stay here it's Christmas day I need to go home." "Sorry but you're not going anywhere for a couple of days."

I remember the doctor asking how I got here and I explained that my friend had dropped me and he's gone home now. I thought I'm not stopping here tonight! They found me a bed and once the dust had settled I sneaked out of the hospital and jumped in my car and drove home arriving back just after midnight. I slept like a log with my hand resting on a chair at the side of the bed, I rang the hospital on Boxing Day and told them I'll come back an hour before the doctor wants to see me!

It took several months before I could use my index finger again, but I'm ever grateful for such a good job they did. Twelve months later I was out poaching with Kaiser using a high powered torch attempting to catch a few hares. He flew at a hare and missed it, then promptly flew back to my fist, only to

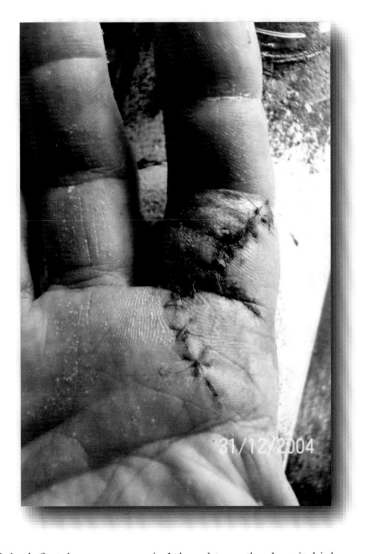

misjudge the glove and hit me full in the face with both feet, here we go again I thought, another hospital job. I lamped for many years with a Harris Hawk catching hares successfully, but I never took Kaiser out again at night. It took me twenty minutes to get him off my face. But I was lucky to escape with just a few scars, could have lost an eye or more!

CHAPTER 6
RABBIT HAWKING WITH KAISER

K aiser had almost twelve months off. The end of his toe had become a lot better and as it wasn't as soft as before I thought it was time to start hunting with him. I had serious doubts as to whether he would be able to catch hares, so I thought I would try him on rabbits first. This was something I would never have done normally as rabbits can be so much easier to catch than hares. The problem I have found over the years with Harris Hawks, Goshawks and even my Tawny Eagle is once the bird is used to catching rabbits they don't want to put in the extra effort required to catch hares. But my goal was to catch a Slovakian hare. I made up a rabbit lure and put it on a long line across the field and used an electric homemade drum to wind in the lure. Kaiser had no problems catching the lure; it was also a great way of getting him fit. His weight was about six and a half pounds and he was well behaved at that weight.

The problem with the electric drum was I could only use it near to the house. I needed something better to use in the fields further away. I came up with the idea of modifying a radio controlled buggy-type car. I bought an electric buggy called Godzilla with twin electric motors, twin batteries and a custom gearbox where the ratios could be changed. Initially it cost me £245.00 but after I had changed motors and gearbox it was nearer £400!

It was very robust and parts readily available, this was not a toy or to be messed with; weighing in at around 12lbs and travelling at 40-50mph you didn't want to be getting in the way of it. I upgraded the suspension, so it could be used on ploughed fields and rough grass.

I took the car body off the buggy and made up a base on which I could fit a stuffed toy rabbit, securing it with Velcro. I made a leather pad and put it on the back of the rabbit so I could attach a piece of meat as a reward for Kaiser. I would drive my car into the field and put the buggy at least 100 metres away hiding it in the long grass.

Then I would open the back of my car and Kaiser's box; initially he would just sit there looking out to see what was going on. I would let him get comfortable for a minute or so, and then by remote, I would start the buggy with the rabbit on. It would shoot off like a bat out of hell! Kaiser didn't hesitate, he loved it once he was on his way. I could turn up the speed and make buggy swerve left and right making it really hard for Kaiser to keep up with it. I always turned it off just as he got there and most of the time he would hit the rabbit so hard it would come clean away from the buggy.

I would give him a minute or two then I would take him back to the car, put him in his box, shut the door and go and set the buggy up for another run. Eventually I could put the buggy at least 400 metres away. I would do this most days getting him to chase the buggy at least a dozen times a day. It didn't take him long to get extremely fit this way. One or two other guys went on to build a buggy using my specification. Mine is about six years old now and I still use it every season. Other guys that I know, with eagles, put a really heavy leash almost like a tow rope and let their birds fly to them with the rope attached. We all have good ideas.

I had lots of good local rabbit land on which Kaiser could hunt. He had been on the buggy for about a month and was extremely fit. It didn't take long for him to start hitting rabbits, but he would let them go very quickly. He was striking with his bad foot first and with the main talon missing this was proving unsatisfactory. He was letting more go than he was catching, and I thought if he couldn't hold a rabbit then he'd have no chance with hares let alone a Slovakian one, which are almost twice the size as ours.

Kaiser used his bad foot first and here he managed to keep a hold of the rabbit. Throughout 2005 -2006 season I kept him on rabbits and at one time I bandaged his right foot up when I took him out so he would learn to strike with his left foot first. I thought this might give him more confidence. He was so enthusiastic but I was worrying he might lose confidence because he kept letting them go. Bandaging his right foot was working, but it was a struggle to bandage his foot some days. I could look at him and think he was saying here we go again more injections, and once or twice he footed me on my un-gloved hand while I was trying to bandage him up. Nothing wrong with his grip as far as hitting my hand was concerned! So throughout the 2005-2006 season I kept Kaiser on rabbits trying to give him the confidence that he would need once he started to hunt hares.

Jim Wood, many years ago up in the borders, used to hate it if his Goldie caught a rabbit; he always had a hell of a job to switch him back on hares. Bob Watkins, who is a great friend of mine, has flown several home bred Harris Hawks over the ten to fifteen years that I have flown with him, and not once has he ever caught a rabbit with them. Correction, I've seen him catch just one. I have though, witnessed him catch over one hundred brown hares and nearly as many blue hares at official club meets. Lots of people I know say their Harris Hawk won't chase hares, but that's because they have caught too many rabbits. Saying all that, John Hall from near Brighton flew a superb male Goldie over the years at rabbits, one of the smallest male Golden Eagles ever flown, I believe. Even today seven years on, Kaiser will still go after rabbits further than he will chase hares.

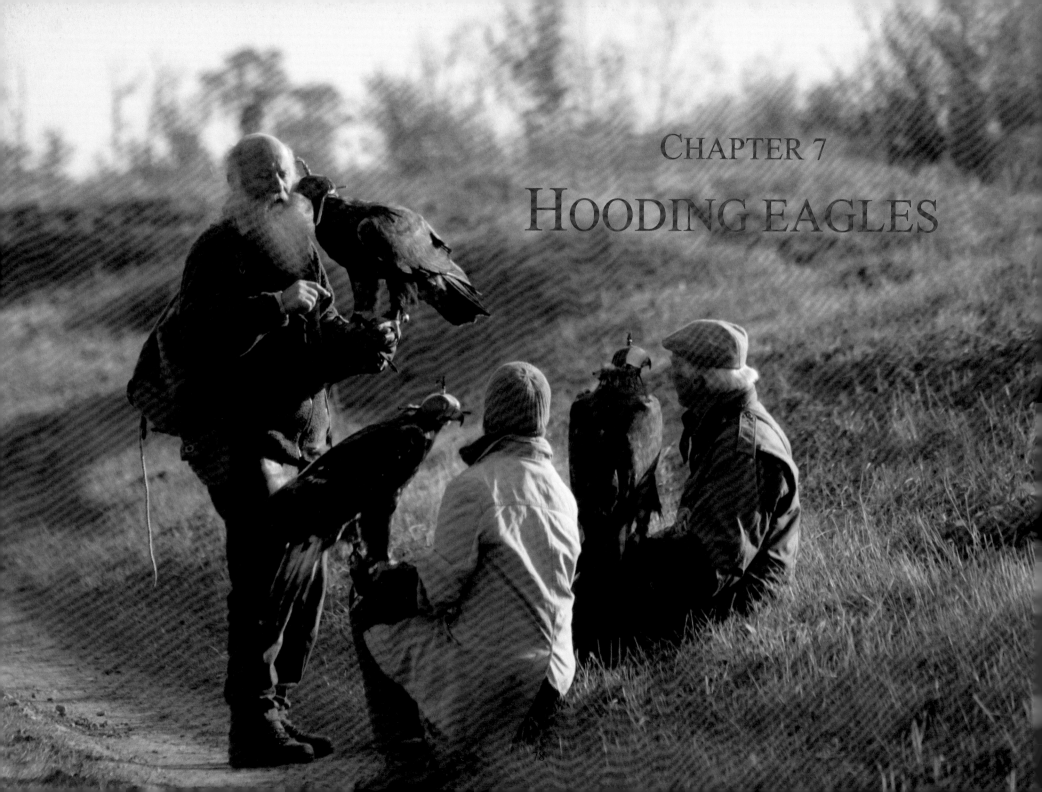

CHAPTER 7
HOODING EAGLES

Eagle hoods are used for a variety of reasons including training, and out hunting. We don't allow eagles to hunt at the same time for their own safety. It is necessary to take it in turns to slip an eagle at the quarry. Also If I didn't hood Kaiser he would take on hares that were half a mile away such was his enthusiasm, however by the time he got there he would be out of energy, so hooding him is favourable. When I get him out of his box, and go into the field and put his hood on; he knows the minute it's slipped off, it's time to start looking for a hare. I also hood Kaiser when we're hunting on our own, to stop him chasing rabbits, which are too easy prey!

Hooding an eagle is also invaluable for fitting new jesses and if it's necessary to be near traffic. Eagles are very calm when wearing their hood. I used to have Kaiser indoors at night when he was being trained to the hood, popping it on and off getting him used to it.

Ronnie with Alex wearing a Romuald slip-on

rderomans@hotmail.fr

The hoods themselves are made from fine leather and are a work of art. There are many different designs originating from different countries where falconry is practised. For eagles, the most favoured hood is called the 'Slip-on' or sometimes the 'Brace-less Hood.' Braces are similar to shoe laces to ensure a snug fit and the hood can be opened and closed by using the leather braces. With slip-ons there are no braces, and they are thought to have originated from the Kazakh region where all eagle hunters are on horseback thus making it difficult to undo a hood with braces. Although they can be undone by using your teeth to pull the braces, when travelling at speed on horseback this can be difficult, so the Brace-less hood evolved. It is great in the field too because it can be taken off your eagle in seconds, necessary when hares spring out from the form and are away at speed.

The disadvantage to a brace-less hood is that there are very few people in the world who can make them properly. They must fit better than a well-fitting glove and at all times be comfortable to wear. If it is too loose the eagle can shake his head and the hood will come flying off, whereas if the hood is too tight it will be uncomfortable for the bird and will be difficult to remove when required.

"I feel qualified to state that Roman de Romuald makes the best eagle slip-on hoods in the world."

Glyn also makes his own superb slip-ons

I made eagle hoods for many years, mainly braced ones. I carved my own wooden blocks to the shape of my eagle's head and then I started to make brace-less hoods. It took hundreds of hours perfecting the shape to ensure a comfortable fit.

I have included one or two of the best eagle hood makers in this chapter.

Because I have made them, and know how difficult they are to make, I feel qualified to state that Roman de Romuald makes the best eagle slip-on hoods in the world. I sold some of my hood designs, by copyright, to one or two well-known hood manufactures, and the Kaiser hood is available from the web. Most of the other makers' eagle hoods are available via emails which I've included, or again from the web. Some of the best eagle hood makers are the falconers who hunt with their eagles. Eventually they end up making their own slip-ons to ensure a comfortable well-fitting hood for their eagles.

Both John Mease and Glyn Thompson make their own excellent slip on hoods for eagles.

Glyn Thompson putting a braced hood on his eagle

81

March 2009

This year we have been fortunate to receive the "KAIZER" hood block from Tom Carnihan. Tom was a well known falconry equipment maker here in the UK and retired recently. Tom developed his Eagle hood block from a male golden Eagle skull and built it up to provide hunting hoods for his eagles. M-J hoods will be digitally scanning this block and reproducing a size range for small to large eagles and then making the "KAIZER" hood (as seen below).

New THE KAIZER

M-J Hoods is also looking into Carbon Fibre hoods for Raptors, having teamed up with a company that manufactures Carbon Fibre products and sharing knowledge with their R&D department. 2009 certainly looks like a year that will produce the first prototype Carbon Fibre COBRA & KAIZER hoods for the world of Falconry.

Some of the eagle hoods I have made from my carved block

John also makes some of the best eagle slip on hoods, in the world.

Extreme Eagle Falconer and Hood maker

John Mease

J M HOODS

83

Mike's Masaai just about to get a beak trim   *Josef Hiebeler's eagles on swing perches*

Putting jesses on an eagle if you're on your own is not advisable, but for me it was fairly easy as I had made falconry furniture for fifteen years or so. Most days somebody would bring a falcon or hawk round to have new jesses fitted. Don't try this at home! Mike Hewlett is photographed with Masaai, his Black Eagle. Look at the size of his feet!

The photo shows the eagle about to have its beak cropped and talons clipped. I don't want to go into too much detail on equipment for eagles, as most eagle owners already have their own preferences, the web is full of falconry furniture manufactures here and abroad. I have however included one or two excellent hood makers for eagle hoods. I made my own eagle hoods for many years, some of which are now mass produced by others. Bow perches and blocks, the choice is again personal preference. I use both and recently there is now a big swing, excuse the pun, for swing perches; they are proving very popular.

Early days at the first ever British Falconry Fair, Althorpe, Northampton. 1994

I made falconry Furniture for a number of years including gloves, hoods, and leather falconry bags.

Here are a few superb eagle hoods made by Ken Hooke in America

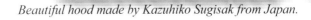

Beautiful hood made by Kazuhiko Sugisak from Japan.

Original Kazakh slip-on hood being held by (Alik) Abylhak Turlybaev

Tom Glacken, excellent up and coming hood maker.

Jeff McKnight

Kaiser's home

People often ask me where I keep my eagle. This is Kaiser's new temporary home, it's approx. 2.5 metres x 3 metres. For the first week I kept him tethered on a long leash, but for the last 5 months he has been totally free lofted and has one perch on the back wall which has a covered roof. He sits up there every night. It has very fine soft netting on roof and he's extremely well manned and doesn't fly around and damage his feathers. In the day time he also comes outside and sits on the lawn and if I get the time he comes in doors for half an hour or so and sits on his indoor screen perch.

Kaiser's home-made box is almost 9 years old and it's my own design. It has cheap wallpaper that runs from the top of box right through underneath where he sits and out the end. This saves putting newspapers in every day. I give it a good scrub at the end of the season and a fresh coat of paint keeping it as good as new. It has carrying handles on both ends and I have old Hoover pipes that I fit through the car's rear window and into air holes, when travelling, to keep him cool.

CHAPTER 8

SCOTLAND 2007-2008

I took Kaiser up to Scotland with Essex boys Bob Watkins, Kevin Parker, Chris Joinison and their Harris Hawks. Kaiser had been catching rabbits for twelve so it was time to see if his footwork was up to catching hares. He was full of enthusiasm for rabbits, so a trip up to Scotland to catch blue hares would be the next step up from rabbits before he went on to the big brown hares that I so desperately wanted him to catch. We were joined by good friend Travis Moles with his big male Golden Eagle. Travis had caught blue hares with his eagle before. We stayed at the Highland Hotel in Newton More, about 20 miles south of Aviemore. We had previously hunted on two estates, Clooney and Kingussie, both have had good numbers of blue hares and over the years we have caught lots with Harris Hawks. This time I was trying it with a Golden Eagle. At least one of the estates has resident breeding pairs of Golden Eagles meaning that Kaiser would only be allowed to fly off the fist at close slips.

In 2007 there was a wild immature Golden Eagle who quickly realised we were putting up blue hares and decided to stay about 100foot above us rather than go hunting blue hares himself. Although this was spectacular to watch we couldn't slip the birds while he was around. He stayed with us for a couple of days, it was a bit unsettling because we knew he was around somewhere but we couldn't see him all the time. I did have one close shave when Kaiser shot after a blue hare we had just flushed, when out of nowhere the juvenile Goldie appeared and decided he wanted the same hare, I have never ran so fast in my life only just getting there in time to make the wild Goldie fly off.

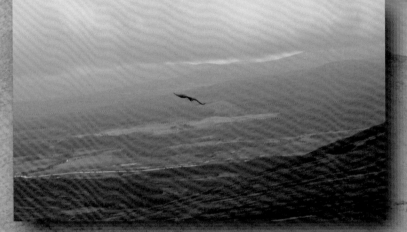

Trav's Goldie waiting on high above Kingussie.

Mr T with his Goldie. Graham the keeper alongside Kevin, Chris and Mr Watkins. Graham would take us right to the top of the estate in his Land rover. We would spend the rest of the day flushing blue hares on the way down. That was providing the weather was good. Some years we would walk to the top if the weather was bad, but that was hard work.

Mr T, Travis, calling his Goldie back to the fist after waiting on a good half an hour, but no blue hares were flushed on this occasion.

Kaiser wasn't interested in the blue hares he only wanted to chase them off. So I would have to wait another year. However I took some fantastic photos and that more than made up for the disappointment of him not catching a blue hare.

Every time I see these photos they remind me of my wonderful mother and how proud she would be.

Kevin Parker's female Harris Hawk on the Kingussie estate nr. Newton More

Middle photo skilfully put together by Bob Watkins, whose graphic skills are unsurpassed.

Chris Joinison's female Harris Hawk Taking a superb blue hare on the Kingussie Estate.

CHAPTER 9

KAISER AND THE FOX

It was mid April and the hunting season had ended several weeks earlier. I was still taking Kaiser out flying on the fields at the back of my house, more for exercise than anything. There were one or two hares on the fields, Kaiser had had several attempts at catching them earlier on in the year but these were well seasoned hares. These hares didn't sit in the form like most hares, they sat upright so they could be spotted a long way off. I used to slip Kaiser a good two hundred yards away he was never short of enthusiasm, but sometimes I used to wish he would mature a bit and use his brains.

I hadn't been in the field very long when something in the middle caught my eye. I stood still for a minute just to see if what I had spotted a few seconds earlier was a hare. As usual, around here, they sit upright. The grass was quite long and all I could see was a pair of ears, or so I thought, sticking out above the grass. I couldn't be sure if it was a small Munjac or indeed a hare. I thought I would take Kaiser's hood off and let him see if he could spot the small pair of ears. The hood was barely off when he started bating towards what I had seen. I slipped him off my fist and within seconds he was away, I knew by watching how fast his wings were beating that he was onto something.

"to my horror it was a fox..."

Within seconds I realised I had made a dreadful error in not clearly identifying the quarry before releasing Kaiser. To my horror it was a fox and not a hare or deer, this was a big, big mistake on my part. As Kaiser was now committed and with one of his big hunting talons missing he could be in serious trouble, I vowed I would never intentionally fly him at fox for that very reason and although it wasn't intentional had I double-checked I would never have released him.

The grass looks to be only three to four inches high yet clearly a very large fox can make his body disappear ,when you look at the photo, and you are now looking at what I thought was a hare not a big fox.

Thankfully both Kaiser and the fox didn't want to take things any further than curiosity. It was Kaiser's first time seeing a fox up close and probably the first time the fox had ever seen a Golden Eagle. The fox probably thought it was a rather big pheasant! I was really pleased there wasn't a scrap as I couldn't be sure Kaiser would come of better than the fox. It really wasn't my intention to fly him at foxes because of his missing main hunting talon.

CHAPTER 10

KAISER'S
FIRST BROWN HARE

At last almost two and a half years after bringing Kaiser from Slovakia he took a hare, in great style at a club meet in Cambridge, on the 24th February 2007. The sense of relief was great, I never doubted him I knew it was just a matter of time. Others had doubted whether I should continue with my goal to catch a Slovakian hare with him. When he lost his big talon, I only doubted how long it would take him to realise that he would have to try and use his other foot to overcome his disability. Now he had the first one under his belt there should be no stopping him. It was good that he caught the hare with all my mates present and I got it on camera. They were all pleased for Kaiser. He was never short of enthusiasm, he always gave his best and so many times he had been kicked off hares because holding them with just one foot makes it easier for the hare to break free and escape.

CHAPTER 11

UK EAGLE FALCONRY

I n this chapter I have included photographs of Eagle falconers that I have met at Eagle meetings and close friends who are also Eagle falconers. There are lots of other Eagle falconers from the UK who as yet I have not had the pleasure of hunting with them and there Eagles.

Go on my son!

Mike, Jamil, Richard and myself at an early Northampton Raptor Club Eagle meet near Weedon

Early days in Revesby Lincolnshire. An eagle meeting organised by me and from where the Uk Eagle Falconry Association was originally founded. We had several more eagle meets from October 2007 through till March 2008 Kaiser did manage to take a couple more hares but was still letting lots go. However he was trying hard and on some of the meets he was averaging only two slips a day, hardly his fault he wasn't catching them.

Top man Roy Lupton. What Roy doesn't know about training Golden Eagles isn't worth knowing

Pete Sibson with Roy And Wesley

Roy Lupton with Rebecca and Robin Moore at the Amesbury Eagle Meet in Wiltshire

Jeff McKnight at Revesby

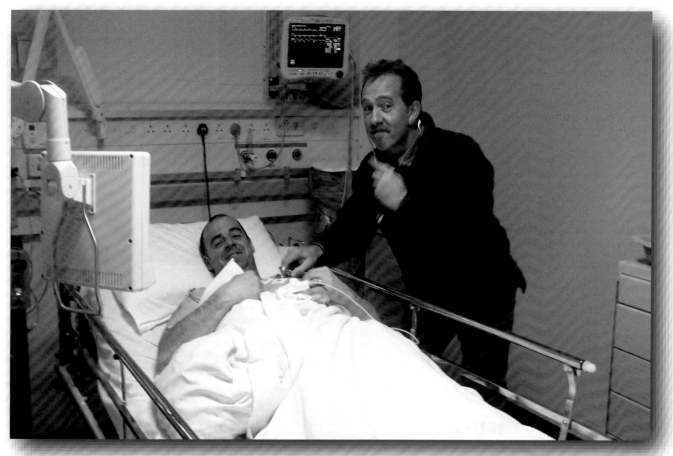

Travis trying to get out of paying the hotel bill, at Kingussie 2008, being examined by Dr Bob Findley

Bill Buck's stunning Bonelli's Eagle (home bred)

My passion for Bonelli's Eagles was sparked over forty years ago when I saw a wildlife documentary about birds in Spain which showed a Bonelli's Eagle catching French Partridge. This bird is sometimes called the Partridge Eagle and does take a lot of feathered game in the wild. The seed was then set. I had been flying mainly Goshawks since my early 20's and had bred Goshawks and Peregrines and more recently Martial Eagles.

Then a friend of mine, Bob Watkins, had put together a pair of Bonelli's Eagles, but these were proving difficult to breed. We had lengthy discussions on how to encourage these birds to breed and after several years, with little interest shown by the birds, a decision was made to position the nest in a different part of the aviary. Finally there was some interest and they nest built and were successful that year. There was only one chick which turned out to be a male that I flew for one season. The next year a female was bred, again I flew this bird for one season. During this period, Bob and I put together another unrelated pair of adult Bonelli's Eagles. This pair settled down very quickly and I managed to breed one young male, who was also flown. The reason that these three youngsters were only flown for one season was that they were needed for breeding projects.

The following season, I finally managed to breed a female that has become my main flying bird. I have been flying Bonelli's Eagles for seven years now and yes, I did make mistakes with the first bird. I find that they are intelligent and once a mistake is made it is almost impossible to rectify.

For instance, when I was training the first male that I flew, I used to get a friend to run along dragging a dead hare which seemed to work very well but, on one particular field meet, there were some people half a mile away and the bird was focused over my shoulder looking at them waiting for them to run. So nowadays I would opt for an electric lure mechanism which drags the dead hare away from you. I also call the bird to the fist for a small reward (chick leg), and not to a lure as some people might suggest as I feel that you are robbing the bird every time you take the bird up off the lure. This is only my opinion as I have never had a problem with calling them to the fist.

I was flying this bird much like you would a Goshawk, unhooded, but I later found out that it is much more controlled slipping the bird out of the hood. Also if you fly a Bonelli's while the bird is unhooded on the fist, the bird will try to take on hares so far away that you could hardly see them yourself. If you slip these hares it is very demoralising for a young inexperienced bird.

My female, who I call Bibi, is now in her fourth year and the bond with me has become stronger with every season. She is not an imprint but there is a definite trust between us. I cannot comment or have the experience on how an imprint Bonelli's would behave as I have only flown parent reared birds.

All in all I have enjoyed flying this species and home bred eyasses are so different from the impressions given in some of the old books written about them. So all in all if you want to fly an eagle and you have sufficient land available and don't want to carry around one of the heavier species, then a Bonelli's Eagle may well suit you.

William Buck

*Cambridge club meet (Fiona's) Bill and Mike with Bonelli's Eagles,
Robin with male Goldie (Odin) and Tracy Murray and Victoria*

116

Holcott Eagle Meet 2008-02-16

The first Eagle meet was held at Holcott in Northamptonshire and organised by myself. It was kindly hosted by Mr and Mrs Harris. Lots of hares running around on the day.

*Lots of spectators starting to gather for the first ever
Holcott Eagle Meeting.*

*Travis, Clint and Roy all travelled from Kent,
with their eagles. A two and a half hour journey*

Richard, from Twin Lakes in Melton Mowbray, at the eagle meeting at Holcott.

William Richard Alldiss from the Sports Agency hosted the first eagle meet of the season for deer and fox.

"Give me the money"

The meet was held just outside Hertfordshire. Strong winds won the day

Mark Dunn with Buttons

Clint at Reed meeting in Cambridge, with his Goldie and also
Ferruginous x Redtail hybrid, bred, I believe, by Bob Crease.

James Bradbury with his Goldie –Steppes Hybrid

Glyn had only flown one Bonelli's eagle and one other Golden eagle prior to getting Otto his current male Goldie and admits that he is still somewhat of a novice as far as eagle falconry goes. However he has been a falconer for forty three years, and has successfully flown most other raptors at quarry in the UK. In such a short time of flying Otto, one can only applaud how much hard work and effort Glyn has put into his bird. In his first season of hunting with Otto he caught just under thirty head of quarry. But in his second season he has caught an incredible 126 head, including brown and white hill hares, rabbits and a couple of foxes.

He regularly takes 2-3 hares in a day and his best to date is four brown hares in one afternoon. Glyn tries to get out as much as possible hunting with Otto such is his passion for hunting with eagles. Glyn also works his German short haired pointer Stan with Otto. No mean feat when you're hunting with eagles, as they can very quickly take a swipe at the dog. However in Glyn's case he has the balance working nicely, and puts down a lot of his success to having the dog on his team. To take 126 head of quarry in your second season with a young eagle has to go into the record books. In over thirty years of flying eagles I have never heard the likes of any one coming close to those numbers especially in the UK.

I've seen it all now.

We must have walked for five hours across ploughed fields without a slip. We were still smiling at the end of the day!

Tom and I only met over the last hunting season, but since that first day we have become very good friends and have been out on a number of occasions hunting with both our eagles together.

So when Tom asked me to write this short paragraph for his new book I felt very honoured. I still consider myself somewhat of a novice as far as eagle hawking goes, although I have been a practising falconer now for over forty years.

Well the time spent flying Hans had certainly wet my appetite for eagle hawking, and for many years afterwards I had dreamt of once again flying another eagle.

I was now fast approaching my fifties and thought that if I didn't do it soon then I never would. So three years ago I purchased my second male Golden Eagle, Otto was hopefully going to be my long term flying companion for the rest of my falconry days. I took my time with him right through our first season together, building up his confidence, manners, and getting him as fit as possible with long lure flights before gradually entering him on his first live hare. Otto took to hunting hares naturally and has gone on from strength to strength over the last three seasons with me. I can't wait for the long summer to finish so we can once again be out on the hunting ground again.

"As for eagle hawking in the UK today, well it's never been more popular."

Well it was around seventeen years ago when I had my first taste of eagle hawking, I had bought a male Golden Eagle that I named Hans. He was a 6 month old imprinted bird from Joseph Hiebeler in Germany; we managed to catch a fair few brown hares in our first season together. However our time was sadly cut short, when I had a bad accident, and partially lost the use of my right arm. This left me with no alternative but to move Hans on to a new owner. Something that I regretted deeply as I've often wondered what we could of achieved if we had more time together.

I can't explain what it is about flying a Golden Eagle or any eagle for that matter. All I can say is that they completely take over your life like no other bird that you will ever own. The only thing I could compare it to would be having a dog, as they seem to know what you're thinking, and the bond that you can achieve is very similar.

As for eagle hawking in the UK today, well it's never been more popular. This in one way is good for the sport as we do need new guys getting into this branch of falconry to keep it alive.

But on the other hand I think some people need to take a step back and think long and hard about what they're getting into.

It's a full time job just getting an eagle fit enough to chase game, you will need at least a couple of good friends to come out daily with you whilst training the bird to chase the lure. You certainly can't fly a bird of this size for two days a week and expect to see the full potential from the bird.

You should also have access to acres and acres of good open land that is well stocked with hares or you will just be wasting yours, and more importantly, the bird's time.

Eagles can be ruined quickly by bad handling just as any other species of raptor. But the difference with a badly trained eagle is in how dangerous it can be compared to the smaller raptors.

I hope that eagle falconry continues to flourish in the UK as it would be a sad day if it didn't. But anyone getting into eagle falconry should realise that it's a long term partnership. Not just a bird for one or two seasons, which can then be sold off to anyone with enough money to buy it.

I cannot see myself flying anything else for the foreseeable future; in fact I have now bought Otto a young girlfriend whom I named Paris. My aim, for the next season, is to get the pair of them out flying together and to compare the difference between the two sexes.

Good Hunting.

Glyn Thompson

Describing my part in British Eagle Falconry, I have been hunting with eagles for some ten years or so. My bird of choice will always be the female Golden Eagle.

Last year, without a female available, I flew a second year male Goldie who took many hares alongside my Albidus Goshawk, Morticia. He flew like a young eagle learning to handle the wind in a very hard season. At five pounds fifteen ounces, he caught deer, fox and many brown hares. He is a very courageous young bird and will become a very good Eagle although I do feel he can be outmatched on deer and fox due to his small size, however, on hares this and his speed is a great advantage.

"Easy is not a word found in the vocabulary of an eagle falconer"

I find this book and its contents refreshing. So often books are works of fiction, written and produced by individuals, pretending to be something they're not. Not so with this book. Tom is a good friend who I first contacted when in search of advice on taking quarry with a Tawny Eagle. At the time, Tom was the only person in the UK who had enjoyed any degree of success with a Tawny Eagle. Tom has just had his best season ever with Kaiser accounting for many brown hares and his first deer. This is no mean achievement and is the culmination of years of hard work. Tom always believed in his eagle and has a special bond with his boy.

Emma was a female Golden Eagle that I purchased at three years old and by the age of five she had become a very proficient hunter. She would take all quarry, including blue hare, brown hare, fox and three species of deer with ease. Basically if she could see the quarry she would fly it down. She regularly took on slips in excess of six hundred metres, in fact the longer the slip the more she seemed to excel. Emma was slipped on deer maybe a hundred times before she took her first. I remember it well, we sat together as she fed on her prey and I felt completely at one with nature. Such moments are etched on the soul and are the reason behind this consuming obsession that is eagle falconry.

The only way to attain success with a Golden Eagle is through hard work, blood, sweat and tears with a little insanity thrown in. Hunting with an eagle is a consuming passion. The bond that is formed with your charge is similar to one you would have with a good working dog, in my opinion eagles are intelligent enough to understand being disciplined.

When I hunt with a Golden Eagle I'm looking for a sense of achievement not a high tally of quarry.

During the 2011 season I found myself without an eagle to fly. I had a large Finnish female and I decided to hunt brown hare with her. She had flown well and it was an excellent season taking many brown hares. Despite enjoying this I felt something was missing. Another eagle falconer, Travis Moles, was in the same situation. He was without an eagle so he bought a female Harris Hawk. On her first meeting with the South East, she caught two brown hares. I also caught two with the Gos, considerable cause for celebration you would have thought? When I asked Travis how he felt, he said it was too easy and afterwards commented that it's not the same without an eagle.

I do not mean this to upset anybody or demean their branch of Falconry, but only to point out that Eagle Falconry is a consuming passion that takes over your life. Once struck down with this illness there is little chance of recovery. It takes five years to bring an eagle to maturity, during this time when you are frozen, soaked and exhausted you wonder for your sanity. Easy is not a word found in the vocabulary of an Eagle Falconer! When the rewards come the feeling of achievement is great.

In this country, there are fewer than twenty or so eagles that are hunted correctly; achieving success on a regular basis is by no means easy. Golden Eagles are not weekend birds, commitment is paramount.

My advice to anyone considering hunting with a Golden Eagle is "don't." Attend a few Eagle meetings, see what's really involved and talk to the right people. In Falconry there are too many so called experts, the answer is clear, when the bird leaves the fist, the talk stops. If you like what you see ask them for advice.

In my early days in Falconry I was lucky enough to meet the right people, including Tom, Roy Lupton and on several trips to Scotland, Neil and John Hunter, I was never short of good advice.

Robin Moore

Myself with great friend Ronnie

Eagle falconry is passion carried out by dedicated few Nowhere are there people more dedicated to the health and well-being of birds of prey than falconers.

The camaraderie between eagle falconers, and the respect they have for each other, has never been better. Trained eagles are never tame; they have over many hours, weeks and sometimes years established a working relationship with their human partners. The ancient and noble art of falconry spans thousands of years. Inherent is a knowledge and understanding of the bird's needs, characteristics and interminable patience to establish a working bond. The late Dr Leslie Brown an eminent scientist/ornithologist rightly described falconry as "the highest form of ornithology". Those not part of the sport may see us as elitist, but this is so not the case. We cherish what we have; always willing to share. We may be guilty of our own success by making the sport look easy and this could mislead would-be eagle falconers.

Watching with amazement, these magnificent birds, attracts people to be a part of it. The expertise of the eagle falconer disguises the enormous effort, hard work and dedication needed to attain success. Eagle falconry is not as easy as it looks. Training and flying other raptors also needs commitment and hard work but the two are very different, it is not an easy or automatic step up to flying an eagle. Eagle falconry is small, even across Europe, compared to other sports, like fishing or shooting mainly due to the commitment involved. However there is a conscious awareness of how easy it could be to lose this sport

Despite this there are always those that threaten the continuation of the sport, by not taking it seriously. It takes respect to stand and applaud an eagle falconer, recognising his achievements, rather than condemn a fellow sportsman. They would then gain the respect they deserve. The culmination of years of true dedication and commitment is realised the moment you slip your eagle and the hunt begins. This sport will survive, because of those that appreciate this.

"The highest form of ornithology"

Thomas Carnihan.

Kajser at Reed Cambridge Eagle meeting 14.2.2008.

GATHERING OF EAGLES

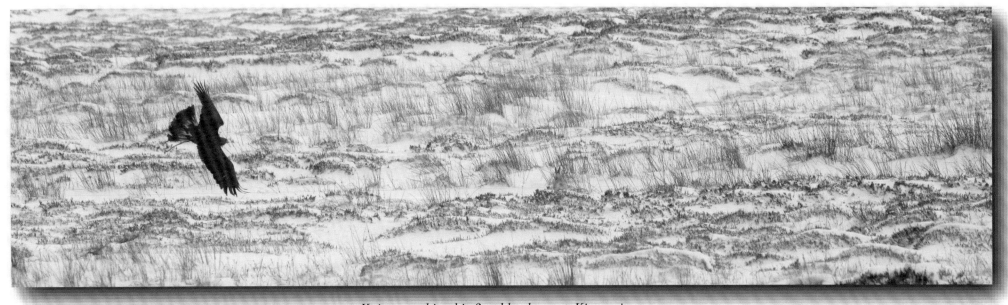

Kaiser catching his first blue hare at Kingussie.

151

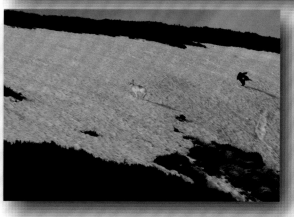

Flying Golden Eagles in Scotland

I was 12 years old when I saw a gentleman called John Murray fly a golden eagle named Samson. It was then that I knew I would fly eagles one day. That was in 1976 and I didn't realise it would take me 26 years to fulfil that dream, or that flying eagles would become the obsession that it has. In November 2002, I purchased "Bentley", a 6 month old untouched male golden eagle from Andrew Knowles Brown. I took my time with him building firm foundations for the future, and he eventually flew loose 12 weeks later, hooding and travelling well with great manners. He showed no aggression towards my dogs and was generally a pleasure to handle and be around.

Waiting on' flying was my aim, and within seven days of his first free flight, I had strong winds on favourable ground that held some brown hares. I, my brother John and my 15 year old son Christopher headed off for the day.

In hindsight, it was probably quite reckless. Although the conditions were perfect, there was a strong wind blowing right up the hill face. I simply un-hooded Bentley and let him go. In no time at all he was about 800ft up, directly above me. He had 2 misses on hares with multiple attempts on each, returning directly above at a good pitch after each. After about 40 minutes he was still directly above me at a very good pitch when hare number three flushed. He stooped vertically, missing the hare, but had learnt in that short time, to throw up to give himself any chance of catching it. From the initial stoop he threw up 3 times, taking the hare really well on the third occasion.

I was hooked from then on and John decided from then that he had to get a golden eagle too.

A day or so after this, I was contacted by Jemima Parry Jones and asked if I would buy Cinnibar, the only young golden eagle bred at the National Bird of Prey Centre from Sabel, Philip Glasiers female. Cinnibar had been bred by artificial insemination in 1998 when Sabel was 32. Sadly Sabel died in 2000.

"I was hooked from then on and John decided from then that he had to get a Golden Eagle too"

I was honoured to be given the chance to own her, and picked her up a few days later. I carried on flying Bentley for the remainder of that season and was able to fly Cinnibar for the last 6 weeks. She took to 'waiting on' flying really well. Despite comments that 'waiting on' flying has minimal success, I found the contrary to be the case. In the weeks I spent in my first season flying in this style, I racked up a very respectable head of mountain hares, with both eagles. I did catch some brown hares, but chose the mountain hare, or Blue hare as it is often called, as my main quarry, as they are the natural prey of the Golden Eagle. I love the places. This type of eagle falconry takes you as you often see wild eagles, and on occasion I have had them fly alongside my eagles. There is also the physical challenge involved. A day on the hill carrying an eagle is certainly not for the faint hearted.

My second season was no different, and again flying Bentley and Cinnibar, I enjoyed great success flying in the 'waiting on' style. It really is the best way to fly golden eagles. Unfortunately that ground was lost for a number of reasons, but no sooner had that happened, than I managed to get access to land closer to home with a good population of mountain hares. The only problem with this land is that it is more undulating and does not lend itself to 'waiting on' flying, so 'out the hood, off the fist' flying was the order of the day. We achieved, and continue to achieve very good results with this style of eagle falconry, but it doesn't come close to those early seasons of 'waiting on'.

In 2004 John bought 'Purdey' a mature Golden Eagle, bred by Andrew Knowles Brown, which he flew for three seasons taking a good number of head and gaining valuable experience in handling, flying and hunting a Golden Eagle. However, John had always wanted to train his own Eagle from young so in 2007 John purchased "Floyd" a 6 month old male golden eagle also from Andrew.

> ## "My plan this year is to train a fresh youngster from this year's batch, hopefully purely for 'waiting on'"

Early training and handling went like clockwork, and Floyd has turned into a very effective hunting eagle, and not only that, from day one has always been very stylish at the end of a flight. I remember in his first season, taking on a slip of several hundred yards in a very strong wind. He kept pumping away, never missing a wing beat. We managed to catch the wingover at the end and when we eventually reached him he had the hare firmly in his grasp. His manners on the kill are also second to none and testament to the amount of work and effort that John has put in.

It's great that we both have the same interest and can spend so much time flying the eagles together. We share ideas and tips and I can see us trying to seek out some more mountainous ground to spend time with the eagles 'waiting on' again. Neil had 298 in one of his early season's with Bently which included a mixed bag of Brown and Blue and Pheasant also unfortunately an unmentionable!

I no longer fly Bentley and Cinnibar as they are now a successful breeding pair and have been for the last four years. I took great pride in flying the first hatched youngster from the pair, Nelson, a big lump of a male flying at 8lb 5oz. He has turned into an extremely good hunting eagle, and is very agile despite his size.

> ## Thing's are looking good for UK Eagle Falconry..."

My plan this year is to train a fresh youngster from this year's batch, hopefully purely for 'waiting on'.

Things are looking good for UK Eagle Falconry and although people do come in and dabble, there are people in it for the long haul. John and I hope to spend many more successful years with our birds.

John & Neil Hunter

Travis is one of the nicest guys I have ever met, but he will kill me for telling this lovely little story. We were up in Kinguzzie hunting with the eagles and it was mid February. On the way back to the Hotel at the end of the day we stopped in the small town for some beer and bits and pieces.

As I was parking I saw Travis going in the jewellers. I suddenly realised it would be Valentines day the following Saturday so I also decided to nip in and by my ex wife a present. As I walked in Travis had got a lovely necklace in his hand and asked "what do you think of this" I told Travis it was beautiful so he bought it and left the shop. I bought a present for Lynda and then drove back to the Hotel. We all got washed and changed and met up in the main dining room for our evening meal. As I sat down I noticed Travis was proudly wearing the necklace he bought earlier. I said "I thought you bought that for the Mrs" "No! I just liked it for myself" he replied…..I must be getting old!

" Trav don't forget the milk this time"

Sečovce is 25km north east of Kosice, in Slovakia. In 2007 a group of us, including Bob, Phil, Clint, Kevin, Jonny, Peter and Mick visited as spectators, before deciding to take a couple of eagles, including Kaiser, out in 2008. We had enjoyed the four day eagle meet hosted by Lubo Engler, a close friend of mine. The hotel accommodation had been superb with great food and splendid evening entertainment. We'd paid less than two Euros for the most delicious home-made pizza, cooked traditionally in an open oven, and for beer less than a euro. Slovakian breakfast had taken a bit of getting used to though, red, green, yellow, peppers and salami!

Ivan with Miro and Golden Eagle, common place to see the eagles bought into the hotels and bars.

Niki Lada!

We had a great time lots, of hare fox and deer were caught. The four days had culminated in a spectacular banquet, the food was delicious; the vodka flowed and all was accompanied by good music including Hani Yousiph Girgis on the bag pipes!

Now the long drive back to Bratislava airport and then the flight home. I was determined to come back out in 2008 with Kaiser and catch one of these big brown hares.

2008 hadn't been going well for Kaiser. Despite learning well and not being short of enthusiasm, he had only caught a couple of hares. Unfortunately the hares were in short supply! Fortuitously I had already made arrangements to drive out to Slovakia this year with Clint Coventry to try and catch Slovakian Hares. We were returning to my good friend, Lubo Engler's meet in Sečovce, and we had also been invited to another eagle meeting near Spišský Hrad Castle. Although this was a Fox meeting and I had already decided I wouldn't fly Kaiser, Clint was going to fly his female so I was hoping to get some great action photos.

We set off for Slovakia at the beginning of November, taking the channel tunnel route leaving a total of 1200 miles to drive to Sečovce. Clint drove all the way with just a couple of stops. The autobahns are not just great roads but also provided really good areas to stop, eat and shower, leaving you feeling fresh to continue your journey.

Although the hotel provided a fenced in weathering for the eagles manned by students throughout the night for security, Clint and I preferred to put ours away at night in their boxes. Enrolment took place on the Wednesday, for hunting on Thursday, Friday and Saturday culminating in a splendid banquet on Saturday evening hosted by Lubo and cooked by his wife Jolana..

Golden Eagle x Steppes Eagle hybrid

One of three Golden Eagles Josef Hiebeler brought to the meeting

Miro Micenko with the smallest Goldie I had ever seen, less than two and a half kilos fat. I still kick myself for not buying it, as it was offered to me for only 2500 Euros.

Kaiser once again having a good chase, close but not close enough !

Kaiser trying hard again

I couldn't help but feel sorry for Clint. For the third time that week he picked his chosen spot and waited for the beaters to hopefully flush a fox or deer towards him, only to have the guy who was clearly a lot further away slip his eagle. Much to his credit, Clint didn't slip his. This happened to me several times at Lubo's meet earlier on in the week. It is very frustrating when there are over a dozen eagles at the meet, you don't get as many bites at the cherry. To have someone slip his eagle when he was not the nearest to the hare is frustrating to say the least. In the UK we take it in turns to draw slips so there can be no mistakes. When a guy with a big female eagle is alongside you all day and is trigger happy it clearly puts you on edge. In the four days I slipped Kaiser no more than three times, but at least I came back with a good eagle. Next time I go back out, I will take a leaf out of Hollinshead's book and stand next to a guy with a small male.

THE
EAGLE HAS LANDED

THE
ANGEL OF THE NORTH

Chapter 13

THE WORST DAY OF MY LIFE

Just a few days before we left to go hawking on the isle of Arran my wife of 34 years told me that she was no longer in love with me and wanted a divorce. That was, and still is a real bombshell; I had no idea she was as unhappy as she claimed to be. It was a struggle for me to go to the isle of Arran. I'm glad I didn't fly Kaiser near the electric power lines because if anything had happened to him. I would have jumped in the sea on the way home! When I got back from Arran my wife had already left. I came home to an empty house. It was fair to say my whole world had just been turned upside down!

As I write this, 3 years later, we have not spoken since. Everything I had lived and worked for had just been shattered into a million pieces. Writing this chapter is still very difficult, but it is an important part of the book.

Because of the break up I became very depressed and I decided to put Kaiser up for sale. I could no longer concentrate on flying him properly; my mind was on too many other things, it wasn't fair on Kaiser. Here was the other love of my life. and I felt I had no choice but to lose him too. I advertised Kaiser on the International Falconry Forum and had lots of takers, but wanted someone who would offer him a good home and somebody who already had hunted with a Goldie. Several weeks later I was contacted by Keith Davies who has a small falconry school near the New Forest. Keith has his own male Goldie, Morgan, but it had suffered some terrible foot problems and was going to need several operations before it would be hunting again. Keith would have the time to devote to Kaiser. I agreed to sell Kaiser to Keith on condition that when his Goldie was back in action, and if he no longer wanted Kaiser, he must offer him back to me first. To this he agreed without hesitation. I was torn and distraught, but knew it was best to let Kaiser go. I had waited twenty five years to have a Golden Eagle, watched him suffer having his big toe removed and now I was selling him. Life can be so cruel sometimes!

Kaiser at Keith Davies just before I left him there.

I will never forget the day I parted with him, the second worst day of my life and both in the space of a couple of months; a double whammy as they say! Keith was a lovely guy and his set up was excellent. I knew when I arrived with Kaiser I had made the right choice, however leaving him there and driving home alone there wasn't a bridge that I crossed that I didn't want to jump off!

For the next 18 months or so I wandered round like a headless chicken not knowing what to do with the rest of my life. Suddenly I came to the realisation that I had to flick a light switch off and tell myself to stop loving and thinking about her. It was time to start again and do something meaningful with my life. I sympathise with every one that's been through a similar experience, it's one of the hardest things to do. Not so for my ex as she had told me that she hadn't loved me for at least five years or so. Wish she had told me that, five years earlier!

Keith with Kaiser

I kept in touch with Keith to find out how Kaiser was, and Keith would ring me regularly to keep me up to date. "Thanks, Keith!" I missed Kaiser terribly, especially having been through so much with him, all the problems he had with his toe. I can't express how thrilled I was the day Keith rang and told me that Morgan was recovering well and offered to sell me Kaiser back. To hear him say those words was really like winning the lottery, I had been severely depressed but it was just the tonic I needed for recovery!

Keith's Goldies Morgan, Sienna, and Saxon

Owner Forest Falconry and Gyr Breeder.com

I went and fetched Kaiser as soon as I could and decided there and then that I would continue my goal of taking Kaiser back out to Slovakia to catch a brown hare. I flew Kaiser for a month just to see how he was behaving and I can honestly say to have him back was such a thrill. I swear he was more than pleased to see me too, because every morning I went out to put him on his bow perch he would chup away at me as if to say "don't ever leave me again!" Some days he would be so affectionate, sitting on my fist, chupping away at me whilst pruning my hair with his beak. After flying him for the month I asked close friend Mike Hewlett, who owns Icarus Falconry at Holdenby in Northampton, if he would look after him at his centre until August so he could moult out, and I tried to set up my photography and printing business.

Mike Hewlett's Falconry Experience
Holdenby, Northamptonshire

Mike with Masaai his Black Eagle

"Mike Hewlett of Icarus Falconry at Holdenby House in Northamptonshire first became interested in the art of falconry at the age of 14 when he spotted neighbour Ray Muttock at local Abington Park in Northampton. Mike introduced himself to Ray who took him under his wing.

Mike's first bird that same year was a male kestrel. He had originally been interested in the sparrowhawks that Ray was breeding but was guided by him to start out with a kestrel. To this day he is not sure that this was the right move.

The sparrowhawks that Ray sold to a guy in Stoke at that time, stood on the fist perfectly relaxed fresh from the aviary, by comparison the little kestrel that Mike and Ray picked up was, in Mike's words, 'vile!'

Mike and I met around this time, introduced by Ray.

In the following years Mike kept three Lanners, Misty who was an amazing little bird who became a super display falcon, and a parent reared pair which were kept at my house and succeeded in breeding in their fourth year.

In time Mike, Ray, Adrian Frost and Richard James and I became friends and spent a lot of time doing shows and displays.

Mike's first proper falconry bird was a male goshawk which did really well in its first season but was tragically killed by a female goshawk in the field in her second season.

In 1999 Mike set up his own business at Holdenby House. He took over an existing falconry centre in much need of sorting out and with the help of Jim Harrower and many other friends he changed the ethos of the centre until it became the centre of excellence it is today. Icarus Falconry runs experience days, courses, hunting days, shows, displays, pest control and a very busy breeding programme.

Mike's favourite bird ever flown is his beautiful Black Eagle, Masaai, who he has flown for a number of years in Scotland. He has caught both hare and rabbit over a 10 year period, not in any huge numbers, but always stunning and spectacular flights. Today Mike flies a Bonelli's Eagle which has just had what he describes as his best ever season hunting hares.

Mike is a charismatic and friendly guy who strives for excellence in both his falconry and displays. He and his small team of staff, volunteers and friends work hard to make his centre the very best it can be and he credits them with much of his success."

Words written by Tracey Murray

Tom Morath with Bonellis Eagle at Holdenby

Workaholic John Miller

Some of the dedicated staff at Icarus Experience. Joe, Pam and Tom

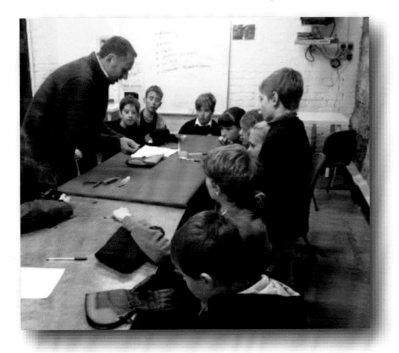

Dave Sharpe from Raptor Exotics. Co-Founder with Tom Morath of the Northampton Young Falconers Club. Seen here with young students, during a falconry equipment lesson.

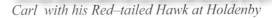

Carl with his Red–tailed Hawk at Holdenby

Pam with a young Barbary Falcon

Not a mention of the F word from this young man,!

Thomas Carnihan

A star in the making, superb commentary all over the bank holiday weekend from Tom Morath from Icarus Falconry at the British Falconers Fair, 2013

Carl gets a rare day off to visit the Falconers fair with partner Sue

Tracy Murray with Elvis

Mike Hewlett, Tom Morath, Tracy Murray and Dave Sharpe from Icarus Falconry

The British Falconry Fair 2013 returns to Althorp House after an absence of 18 years

I contacted a good friend of mine, Lubo Engler in Slovakia, and asked him if I could go over at the beginning of the hunting season with Kaiser and stay for several weeks. He replied very quickly to say I was more than welcome and could stay as long as I wanted.

Lubo is a lovely guy who had come to Scotland with his friend Miro Micenko several years earlier to hunt blue hares with us in the Cairngorms. Since then we had gone to his eagle meetings almost every year since 2000 to either spectate, or as we did in 2008, to try and catch a brown hare with our own eagles. Lubo offered to rent a house for me but I decided I would buy a caravan big enough to live in and big enough to accommodate my large printing machine. I thought that if I was going to go hunting out there with Kaiser I would take some photos to print and sell them at the eagle meetings. I arranged with Lubo that I would go out to Slovakia, after the bank holiday show in August at Stow Cum Quy in Cambridge. I'd taken Kaiser here every year with the SEFG. In the meantime I looked for a suitable caravan that would have room for a six-foot canvas printer, no easy feat; eventually I found one that suited my requirements!

It wasn't long before the end of August came round. I had fitted the caravan with alarms and a couple of heavy duty safes, bolted to the chassis, to hold my camera equipment, passports and, more importantly, Kaiser's paperwork. I gave the caravan a test weekend at the Stow Cum Quy country fair, all went well and I was ready to depart on the ferry crossing that I had booked for the middle of the week.

Departure day came, I'd picked up Kaiser from Mike's. I asked, was it a twist of fate that the last person I saw, by chance as I left Northampton on my way to Dover was my ex-wife on her horse Gypsy. Yet again she turned her head and chose to ignore me. Several hours later as I stood on the upper deck of the ferry watching the lights of the UK dim into the distance. My thoughts turned to sadness. Sadness that one person can be so cruel to another. Sadness that I had to accept that thirty four years of marriage was really over. This is a sadness that will never leave me, haunting me to this very day.

I realised that I needed to concentrate my thoughts towards the new challenges that were taking me to Slovakia.

Photo of my large canvas printer fitted in my caravan bedroom, with a canvas printed photo on the blind.

Caravan just about fitted out in readiness for trip.

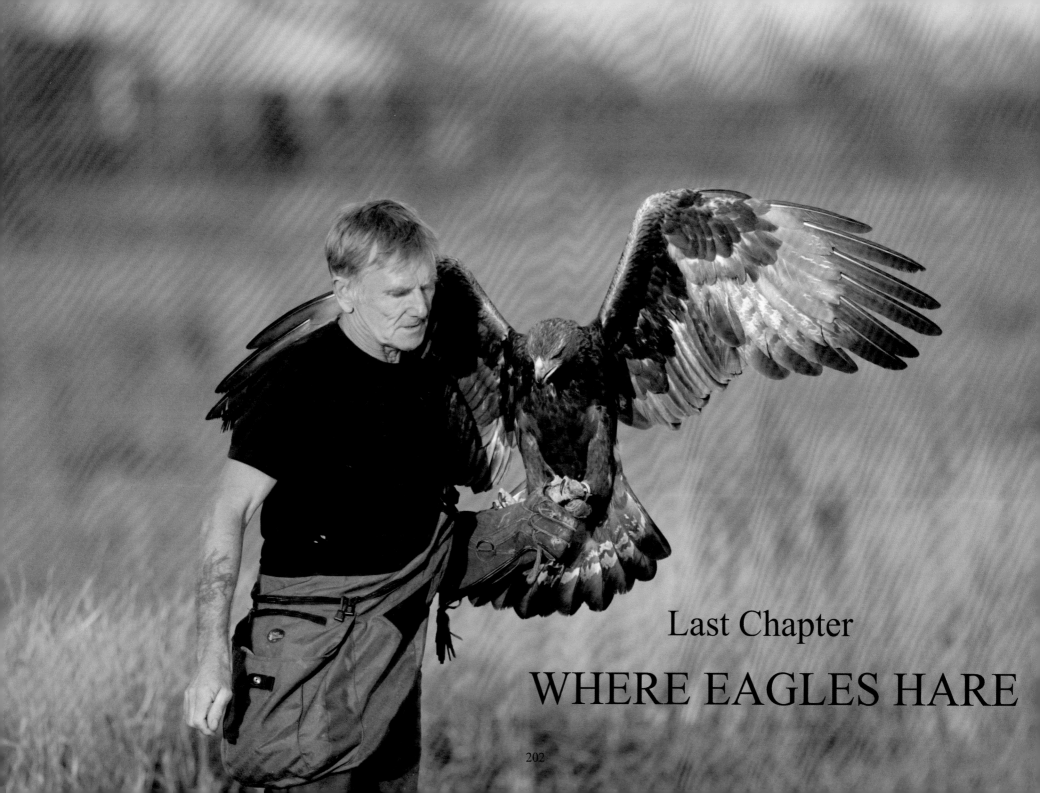

Last Chapter

WHERE EAGLES HARE

New Hotel at

For now I could forget the last couple of years and how dreadful life had turned out and get on with my goal, to catch a Slovakian hare with Kaiser.

Sitting on the ferry, watching the lights of Dover dim in the distance, I suddenly realised I was about to drive 1200 miles on the wrong side of the road towing a 22ft caravan! having never driven on the right before.

I had arranged to meet Lubo in mid Slovakia at a place called Banska Bystrica for a two day festival. Many Slovakian falconers would be there with their eagles and falcons. The weather was great, crowds were big and the festival had a lovely atmosphere.

Lubo Engler

I did eventually get to the festival unscathed although I had one major problem going up a single lane mountain pass as my 'sat nav' sent me the wrong way and I met a petrol tanker coming down. There was no room to pass and I was not about to attempt to reverse down the tricky mountain road towing my caravan. I made the petrol tanker reverse for about half a mile or so much to the annoyance of the 25 cars that were behind it! Here's where I learnt my first set of Slovakian phrases. "Xxxx off you lousy English driver and xxxxxxxx don't come here again!!" This was repeated many times during the next two hours! It was at this point I envied the ostrich, oh to stick my head where the sun doesn't shine! The Slovaks are lovely people really!

The very beautiful Jolana Engler

Martin Engler

Banska Bystrica Festival

Lubo Engler

204

At the end of the festival I continued my journey, following Lubo back to his house in Sečovce. This was about another 150 miles further east. Slovakia is a very beautiful country heavily wooded with lots of wildlife, making the journey enjoyable.

Lubo suggested it would be easier to put my caravan in his garden rather than at his other house, which was great as it meant I had some company. I nearly wrote the caravan off turning into Lubo's garden though, as there was only about an inch each side between the caravan and the iron gates. I was doing about twenty miles an hour when I turned in because I had a couple of big artic trucks behind me, doing about sixty miles an hour, I really thought they were going to take me out.

Caravan safely in Lubo's garden

No health and safety out here!

" Is that straight enough?"

So this would to be my home for a while and we quickly got Kaiser settled in Lubo's garden, which was full of aviaries. Lubo had a couple of his own hunting Golden Eagles, some pairs of Harris Hawks and other falcons. I was very quickly made to feel welcome by Lubo's wife and his two sons, Martin and Lubo junior. The start of the hunting season was about a month away, and I wanted to spend time getting Kaiser fit and settled in. Lubo built everything with a chainsaw, box of nails and a hammer, no spirit levels out here. Lubo went off to Kazakhstan with his friends for three weeks so I got busy building some aviaries for him. The trouble was I forgot how big Lubo was and I built all the doors to the aviaries a little small. When he got back he was really pleased, until he went in the first one and smashed his head on top of the door frame. As soon as he came round he proceeded to chase me round the garden throwing anything he could get his hands on at me including a big hammer! After that he didn't speak to me for a week!

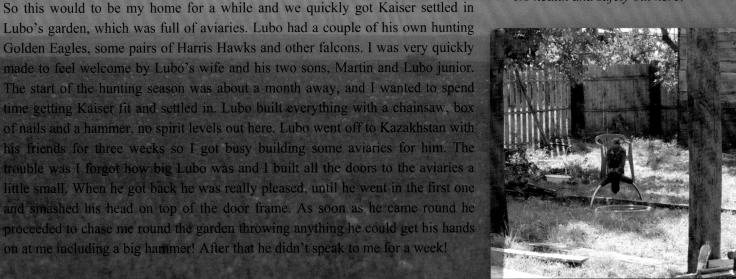

207

Kaiser chasing a roe deer at one of the meets.

One of the biggest changes, I had to get used to, was eating at least four meals a day. In the past twenty years I'd only ever eaten one meal a day at around 8pm at night after my ex came in from horse riding. When I arrived I was just a tad over eleven stone. At the end of my stay, three weeks which turned into three months I weighed thirteen stone, never have I eaten so much food. Seven o'clock in the morning breakfast was cold salami, lettuce, red and green peppers and bread with no butter washed down with hot black tea. Home-made cakes at eleven with milky coffee. One o'clock was lunch of home-made soup, potatoes, hot sausages and more cakes then four o'clock and more lovely cakes and milky tea. Around six came the main meal, soup, more potatoes, goulash, bread, home-made pancakes and jam and more tea. Later in the evening, we had chocolates and more tea. Lubo's wife was an excellent cook and worked non-stop cooking, feeding the family, myself and the dogs, cleaning the runs, doing all the house work and the washing and ironing. In all the time I was there she never sat down once without sewing up a sock or doing the ironing.

Late in the afternoons I would take Kaiser about four miles up the road and fly him on the training fields to get him fit for the meetings. There was a problem with the training ground as it was covered in very long Pampas type grass up to four foot high, and the odd one or two hares that were on there were extremely difficult to see. There were, however, roe deer, and Kaiser was just amazing. He would chase them for miles, he didn't need any training on dragged deer. If I put up a couple of deer, they were usually in twos or threes, Kaiser would be off like a shot, getting fit chasing them. Over the month or so I was on the training ground he managed to bring down at least six. He didn't have the weight behind him to keep them down though. On some days he would ride on top of them for so long before actually catching hold that he would end up 4oo yards away; and by the time I got there with all my camera gear he had either let go or had been kicked off. However, he wasn't put off, every day he would go off and hit another one. Several times I got within feet of getting hold of one, but as soon as the deer saw me they would put in a huge effort to get back up and run with Kaiser still bound to the deer.

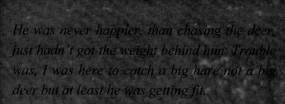

He was never happier, than chasing the deer, just hadn't got the weight behind him. Trouble was, I was here to catch a big hare not a big deer but at least he was getting fit.

For a Golden Eagle that only weighs a little over six pounds he has got a lot of bottle. He didn't back off, no matter how big they were and some of them were really big!

210

There was one occasion when one of the deer, no doubt 'peed off' with this tiny Golden Eagle attacking them every day, decided after being chased for a hundred yards or so that he had, had enough, and stopped! He turned round and ran straight back at Kaiser who was, by this time, flying about four foot off the ground, at about thirty miles an hour. Wham! Kaiser hit him straight on the head. I was taking photos at the time, he needed help and I was two hundred and fifty yards away. I dropped my camera and ran. There was one hell of a scrap, Kaiser had the deer by the throat and the deer was on its back screaming its head off. There was dust everywhere, the deer kicking its legs all over the place. As I was running I was worried that if the deer rolled over it would probably kill Kaiser. For a Golden Eagle, that only weighs little over six pounds, he has got a lot of bottle. He didn't back off, no matter how big they were and some of them were really big! Kaiser was fine, but it took me nearly two hours to find my camera as the grass was over four feet tall. My camera lens cost three thousand pounds, boy was I pleased to find it? After this last incident with the deer I vowed I would not take photos but would run straight away if he needed help. I'd set myself the goal of Kaiser catching a Slovakian hare and not a Roe Deer, Kaiser hasn't got the weight behind him for the big Roe Deer and try as he may he would end up getting hurt. The big brown hares were very difficult to see let alone catch, especially on the training ground. There were plenty of hares on the ground where Lubo would be holding his big eagle meet at the end of the month, but he didn't want me going on there for a couple of weeks catching them, can't say I blamed him. Also I wanted him to catch one at Lubo's meet. The last hare he caught was back in the UK in February and it wasn't anywhere near the size of the hares in Slovakia.

Last time I take photos, from now on I will run and help him

Now I'll take my life in my hands and tell you a funny story, if Lubo ever translates this he will kill me!

While Lubo was in Kazakhstan with his friends, as well as building aviaries I also fed all his birds of prey. I noticed all the baths for the birds, had been turned upside down in their aviaries, so clearly they didn't have any drinking water! (I later found out that clean drinking water is a premium and is bought to the houses via a tanker, no wonder Lubo used to throw things at me while I was cleaning the car and caravan) The weather was scorching hot and I felt sorry for the birds so I connected up a long hose pipe and went round filling all the baths in the aviaries.

Lubo had a massive female Golden Eagle and the bath was right at the back of her aviary, I thought I'm not going in there she might grab me. The bath was turned the right way up but empty, so I put the spray nozzle on the end of the hosepipe and turned it on to full jet force. I poked about two foot of hosepipe through the aviary netting and was trying to aim it at the empty bath, but it was flying round like a snake charmer's Cobra. Suddenly the Goldie flew off its perch. It must have also thought the hosepipe was a snake because in less than a second it had grabbed it and was flying round the aviary with it grasped firmly in its talons. I let go of the hosepipe and the Goldie was now singing its head off, flying round with about twenty foot of hose, the water spraying everywhere. It dropped the hose, but the water was still making it fly around. It attacked the hose again, there were now holes all over the hose and jets of water were spraying everywhere. The Goldie, completely soaked, was still screaming its head off and I was hypnotized, I couldn't move for laughing, I had never seen anything so funny! I pulled myself together and ran and turned the water off. When I got back the Goldie had got the nozzle off of the hosepipe it must have thought it had killed the snake, so I pulled the hose out of the aviary. This upset the Goldie because it must have thought it had been rejuvenated and it flew up to the netting and grabbed the hose again just as I was pulling it clear, so I left it in there for the Goldie to attack. I left it alone for twenty minutes, but as soon as the Goldie saw me coming back it flew at the aviary netting with such force I thought it was going to rip the netting open .

"I used to wake up in the middle of the night in a cold sweat, and all I could see was those piercing yellow eyes"

It had obviously associated me with the hosepipe and it wouldn't let me near. I went back during darkness and pulled the hosepipe clear and I swear the bugger knew I would be back, because the second I started to pull the hosepipe it was on the aviary netting screaming at me. For the next couple of weeks if I went anywhere near the aviary the eagle would smash into the netting at the front of the aviary with such power I thought it's only a matter of time before it gets out and then it's going to kill me! I used to wake up at night in a hot sweat thinking it's got out and was coming for me, especially as the netting was plastic and stitched together in the middle with cable ties. I didn't trust it! The Goldie was a good fifteen to sixteen pounds if not more and its talons were huge. It never forgot me, going for me every time I went past. When Lubo came back from Kazakhstan I made a point of not going near the aviary otherwise he would go berserk wondering what I had done to upset the eagle so much. About a week later we were working on one of the other aviaries when Lubo asked me for the hammer and I went all the way up to the house to get one rather than go near the Goldie's aviary! He suspected something was amiss and when I came back with the other hammer he grabbed me by the hand and took me over to the Goldie's aviary, who by this time was hanging on the front of the aviary screaming at me. Lubo pointed to the back of the aviary and said something not very nice in Slovakian, he was pointing at the nozzle of the hosepipe which was still in there. He then started to undo the front of the aviary door, at this point I did a runner! I thought he wanted me to go in and get the nozzle, I was off! It never forgot me. It didn't help that for the next couple of months every time I did something he didn't like Lubo would try and drag me down the garden making out he was going to throw me in the aviary with his Goldie.

We'd planned to go to an Eagle meeting about three weeks later and Lubo said he was not happy about the way his young Goldie was hunting so he was going to take the big Goldie and fly that at the meeting (unbeknown to me he was joking). I didn't sleep a wink for two weeks, I seriously considered going home early rather than go to a meeting with his big Goldie trying to kill me the minute he let it loose!

In September 2011 we were driving to Poland from Slovakia, to pick up a big female Saker Falcon, which had been shot and was currently being cared for in a veterinary centre. A wild Golden Eagle that had been circling above the car suddenly went into a deep stoop and put up a big brown hare in the field. The hare was running straight towards the road and I thought it would be hit by our car. The hare was jinking violently left and right in an attempt to throw off the eagle, but the eagle was well versed and

had other ideas. It caught the hare less than twenty metres from the road. Even today I can still picture the dust being turned up from the eagle's wing tip as it turned on its side just before its huge talons caught up with the hare. It was absolutely incredible, never in my life did I ever expect to see a wild Golden Eagle catch a hare. I had driven over 1500 miles with Kaiser to catch a hare, and right there in front of me I had been given a lesson in how to do it. Amazing! It was so close but such a shame that I didn't have my camera with me, a memory that will stick with me forever. Lubo wouldn't stop the car he simply said that today you will see that many times. Unbelievably he was right! By the end of a 250 mile trip I gave up counting the number of eagles, I witnessed, hunting.

When Lubo was working, I also helped out by taking a Golden Eagle to the veterinary college in Kocise where Lubo's friend and state vet Ladislav Molnar worked. The Golden Eagle belonged to a falconer in Austria and had a broken leg. Such are the veterinary fees in Austria, falconers shuttle the birds into Slovakia so they can be treated a lot more cheaply. Lubo and other falconers look after the birds locally till they have recovered and then they are shuttled back from where they came. The veterinary college students come to Lubo's eagle meetings to learn more about the birds they are often treating. They thoroughly enjoy their time out in the field and the end of the week banquet!

Big female Saker Falcon, now on the road to recovery after having a bullet removed from her chest.

Whilst I stayed with Lubo we spent some time on a vineyard that was owned by one of his friends. They made Tokaji wine which is one of the finest Slovakian wines. We flew the hawks to scare away the small birds that were eating the grapes. The weather was superb and scenery was stunning.

Martin with his home bred Harris Hawk

Young Lubo with his Sparrow Hawk used for scaring the birds at the vineyard

In all of the three months I stayed in Slovakia, I didn't need anything more than a tee shirt. The weather was fantastic right up to the beginning of December.

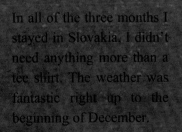

THC 2007

Kirsten Rohloff

Miro Mozola

222

Large dog fox taken by

Jicha Vaclavs' Eagle.

This should have been Kaiser's slip but it wouldn't be fair with his big hunting talon missing. Got some stick from the beaters, when I got back to the hotel, as they had made the fox come out directly where I was standing; until I explained about his missing talon.. Then they apologised.

Kaiser trying hard but still not got one.

Couldn't help feeling sorry for him some days, slips at hares were few and far between. He would fly back to the fist and stomp his feet on my glove to pent out his frustration.

Sometimes he would come out of a good rough and tumble with a hare, shake himself down, get his breath back and go and chase the hare again. The hare, by now was a good two hundred yards away but he put in another good attempt only to be kicked off or just miss. The hares out there are so well versed at evading capture from eagles. I knew it was a case of the more slips he got the more chance he had of catching one, problem was they love fox and deer meetings. Some days, I could understand why.

Thomas Carnihan

231

Thomas Carnih

Kaiser still struggling to get a grip on one of these crafty hares.

We only had Lubo's eagle meeting left and then I would be heading back to the UK. The meeting was in and around Sečovce. I had spent several weeks, with Lubo, feeding pheasants and putting up tall deer hides on all the local land and was looking forward to his meeting. I had been before, with Kaiser in 2008, but didn't catch a hare, and had been a spectator many times with Bob Watkins and Phill Huzzy. It was always well attended with some of Europe's top eagle falconers. It was a great meet for roe deer as well as the difficult to catch brown hare. So my hunting season with Kaiser was drawing to a close. There was only one more meet and then I would be making my way back to the UK. Originally I had planned to stay a lot longer but the language was becoming a problem. Kaiser had only less than half a dozen slips at hares in all the time I had been out here, so if he was going to help me achieve my goal he only has a few days in which to do it. I knew Lubo's meeting held lots of hares, and although Kaiser was fit after spending weeks chasing deer, these were hares that had been hunted by eagles almost daily, but I kept my fingers crossed.

We only had Lubo's Eagle meeting left and then I would be heading back to the UK.

The wine flowed freely!

Only a couple of days before Lubo's meeting, Bob Watkins rang me from London to say he and half a dozen falconers would be coming out to the meet to spectate, and give Kaiser a much needed boost. That was great news to know my mates were coming to the meeting, so now it was a mad dash to sort out picking the boys up from the airport, which can be a nightmare because of the language barrier. They arrived with just a day to go before the meeting started and we got them safely settled into the hotel. Lubo decided we would spend the next day at the vineyard where I had been flying Kaiser. We all headed to the wine cellar at Lubo's normal 90 mph. The famous vineyard, in the Tokaj region, had a massive cellar full of great wooden casks. We were led through tunnels to one cellar where long tables were laid out with lots of bread , dripping and fresh onions. No cheese here but the wine flowed!

Ian, Bob and Kevin knocking back the vino

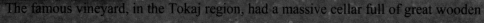

Despite it never being a good idea to get wrecked the day before a meet it was eleven o'clock in the morning and we all had about ten full glasses of red and white and a couple of glasses of 'esso blue' and staggered our way out of the cellar and back to the cars. Lubo drove most of the forty km return journey on the wrong side, the wheels never touched the road, he flew! We all arrived back at Lubo's for tea and to start the vodka session......

Although primarily an eagle meet, it was good to see so many young falconers at the meeting with Goshawks

Looking not too bad considering we were up most of the night drinking vodka. It was great to see so many young faces at the meet, things have gone a bit stale back in the UK as far as newcomers are coming into falconry, here it's all looking very healthy

"Did you see that dog? It just peed up my leg!"

Time to put him in the car and make my day

My kind of falconer!

Kaiser has an early slip, but the hare was too strong

243

Lubo Engler's eagle on his home meet finding it difficult, what hope had Kaiser got?

"HARE" shouts a spectator

In Slovakia, the rules are that the falconer who is nearest the hare when it gets up and runs, slips his eagle first and shouts "EAGLE" to let the others know an eagle is free. It's at this moment the adrenalin starts pumping, because you never know if, in the next second or two, it might be your turn to un-hood your eagle, ever mindful that the guy who is standing less than thirty feet from you has a big female eagle on his fist. He is just as keen to let his eagle go if, in the blink of an eye, a hare gets up. If we both let our eagles go at the same time Kaiser would come off worse, so I always got pretty wound up when I first started walking out. UK rules are different we draw lots to see who goes first; out here it's almost a free for all!

In a split second I shout "EAGLE" a spectator has already seen the hare jump out of the form as it makes it break straight down the middle of the field. I immediately knew it was my slip as the hare was directly in front of me. Without a passing thought to what the guys each side of me are doing, Kaiser's hood is off and he's slipped straight at the running hare.

" Go on my son" I shouted as Kaiser's wings are beating furiously, he wants this hare. You know the second you release your eagle and it spots its quarry whether it's interested or not, boy does he want this! There was a real sense of urgency as Kaiser starts to close in on the hare. Now the hare has several choices, it knows there's an eagle closing in and to avoid capture it has to make a split second decision. If it gets it right it lives to fight another day if it gets it wrong it's 'Goodnight Irene.' My photos show how the hare can avoid capture, they can jump almost six feet in the air, stop on a sixpence and do a complete turnaround in an instant. They can also stop dead and let the eagle overshoot, or they can turn left or right, jink, again in less than a split second. I had started to take photos of the hare, but I could see this was a big one and knew if Kaiser could catch him he would need a hand, so I stopped taking photos and started running.

One of the spectators Viktor Wercholák took some photos and captured my eight year-long goal to catch a Slovakian hare. Kaiser quickly caught up with the hare and carried on, going straight over the top of him. He flew almost vertically and did a complete one hundred and eighty degree turn to meet the hare head on. It was all over in a few seconds, the hare jinked to the left at the same time Kaiser also made the right decision to wing over to his right and caught the big hare clean on the head. This was a really big hare and it was now fighting for its life to break free. Kaiser was changing his grip to try and stop the hare kicking him; they can easily break the eagle's leg or wing with a powerful kick. I ran to try and catch the hare but it was pulling Kaiser all over the place. Every time I got close the hare pulled Kaiser further away. After what seemed an age, the hare started to tire and Kaiser was slowly managing to hold it. I quickly dived on the two of them and it was all over. Kaiser had caught his first Slovakian hare and it was all captured as photos by Viktor. I was over the moon, all my best mates had flown out to the meet and right in front of them Kaiser had caught a Slovakian hare, and I was even more thrilled because he had caught it at Lubo Engler's eagle meeting.

Bloody Hell "RODNEY! He's only gone and got one"

Kaiser with his goal, needless to say he had a really good feed when we got back to Lubo's. At the end of the meet, on the Saturday night before everybody went home, the Slovenska Club put on a great evening's entertainment for all the falconers and spectators. Lots of food and drink and some good times were had. I wasn't able to return out in 2012, but have already started to make arrangements to go back out in November 2013 with Kaiser and catch another hare.

I would just like to say a very special thank you to Lubo and Jolana for looking after me so well, it had been a difficult time for me and they went out of their way to make me most welcome, two years on and I still miss Jolana's cooking and lovely cakes.

So here it was, the end of my eight year goal to catch a Slovakian hare, what a day!

After the removal of his main hunting toe and talon, others were prepared to write Kaiser off, but I was never going to confine him to an aviary. Twenty five years of wanting a Golden Eagle I was determined to give him the best possible chance to hunt. At my lowest point, I'd parted with him, but his return was the inspiration I needed to give my life purpose again. Together we achieved the challenge of him catching a Slovakian hare, and the last hunting season (2012) was his best ever. I'm now fulfilling my ambition of publishing the story. My next goal, with the help of other eagle falconers, is to host an international eagle meet here in the Fens. Plans have already begun for 2015.

Pictures from the book are available as mounts and framed pictures, from the website, www.whereeagleshare.com

To see Kaiser hunting, arrange a day out with Tom Carnihan via the website, www.whereeagleshare.com

To all my Slovakian friends…

After a long and happy marriage that ended rather abruptly in September 2009 I struggled for some considerable time to come to terms with it. Slowly I started to rebuild my life, but during the early part I regretfully sold Kaiser, a demonstration of the fact that I wasn't myself. The turning point came when I was given the opportunity to buy him back and it was just the tonic I needed.

Close friend Bob Watkins had spoken to Lubo, via good friend Natalie who did all our interpreting for us. Lubo told Natalie to tell Bob that I was welcome in Slovakia anytime I wanted to go.

So I decided I would take Kaiser out to Slovakia for the 2011 hunting season. The camaraderie between the Uk and Slovakia had never been better, as for almost ten years we have been going out to Slovakia to spectate or take part in the Eagle Meetings. I had a wonderful time during 2011 hunting with some great people. I think Lubo Engler and one or two others have played a tremendous part in bringing us all closer together and they should be applauded for what they have done.

I would like to say a special thank you to the Engler family for taking me under their wing, an almost complete stranger, and showing me such a great amount of hospitality. They allowed me to put a really big caravan in their garden and Lubo's charming wife fed me almost to the point of bursting with her lovely home cooking including some wonderful cakes. Lubo has two fine sons who also treated me with great friendship. Lubo speaks very little English and my only Slovakian was "do bray do bray." The two boys helped me understand what I did wrong especially when some days Lubo would chase me round the garden throwing anything he could get his hands on including hammers and bricks. I built some new aviaries for Lubo's eagles while he was in Kazakhstan but I forgot how small I am and how big Lubo is, I was thrilled when he came back and said "fantastic I'm so proud of you for what you have done." That soon changed when he opened the aviary door and knocked himself clean out on the door frame.

We had some fun times; I just hope he doesn't kill me when he reads about the hosepipe incident in the last chapter. They showed great patience and kindness to a stranger at a time when I needed it most. That is something I will never forget. It shows how great Eagle falconry is in Europe.

Lubo is a very hardworking and a proud man; I spent many days with him in the forest dragging trees down treacherous slopes that only the foolhardy or the brave would tackle. His tractor would be better suited if it were in a museum, and yet he could drive it up mountains where no others would dare to go. Sometimes he would make me and a friend sit on the front of the tractor to add some weight to the front while he drove the tractor up the slippery mountain track purely on its back wheels. Evel knievel eat your heart out, you aint done nothing compared to the risks this guy took, every day, just to put a meal on the table for his family. Long may our friendship continue to flourish. Thanks again to the wonderful hospitality that you showed to me, and for allowing me to 'live the dream' and complete my goal of catching a Slovakian hare with Kaiser.

Your great friend,

Thomas Carnihan.

Všetkým mojim priateľom zo Slovenska...

Po dlhom a šťastnom manželstve, ktoré skončilo dosť náhle v septembri 2009, som sa snažil dosť dlho vyrovnať sa s tým. Pomaly som začal znovu budovať svoj život, ale na začiatku som žiaľ predal Kaisera, čo dokazuje, že som to jednoducho nebol ja. Zvrat prišiel vtedy, keď som dostal príležitosť kúpiť ho naspäť, a to bolo povzbudenie, ktoré som potreboval.

Blízky priateľ Bob Watkins sa porozprával s Ľubom, prostredníctvom dobrej kamarátky Natálie, ktorá nám všetko tlmočila. Ľubo povedal Natálii, aby dala vedieť Bobovi, že som na Slovensku vítaný kedykoľvek, keď sa rozhodnem ísť.

A tak som sa rozhodol, že zoberiem Kaisera na Slovensko na loveckú sezónu 2011. Kamarátstvo medzi UK a Slovenskom nebolo nikdy lepšie, nakoľko posledných 10 rokov sme chodievali na Slovensko pozerať sa alebo sme sa aj zúčastňovali organizovaných stretnutí s dravcami a ja som zažil počas loveckej sezóny 2011 fantastický čas s niekoľkými super ľuďmi. Myslím si, že Ľubo Engler a jeden alebo dvaja ďalší zohrali obrovskú rolu v zblížení našich krajín a mali by sme ich pochváliť za to, čo urobili.

Rád by som vyjadril špeciálne poďakovanie rodine Englerovcov, za to že ma prichýlili pod svoje krídla, mňa takmer úplného cudzinca, a preukázali mi takú veľkú dávku pohostinnosti. Dovolili mi postaviť môj naozaj veľký karaván do svojej záhrady a Ľubova šarmantná žena ma kŕmila až takmer do prasknutia svojou vynikajúcou domácou kuchyňou vrátane fantastických koláčov. Ľubo má dvoch milých synov, ktorí sa ku mne správali veľmi priateľsky. Ľubo hovorí len málo anglicky a jediné, čo viem ja po slovensky, je „do brav do brav" dobre, dobre. Tí dvaja chlapci mi pomohli pochopiť, čo som urobil zle, hlavne v niektoré dni, keď ma Ľubo naháňal po celej záhrade a hádzal po mne všetko, čo mu prišlo do ruky vrátane kladiva a tehál. Postavil som nejaké nové voliéry pre Ľubových orlov, kým on bol v Kazachstane, ale zabudol som, aký som ja malý a aký veľký je Ľubo a bol som vo vytržení, keď sa Ľubo vrátil a povedal „fantastické, som hrdý na teba, čo si dokázal." Toto sa čoskoro zmenilo, keď otvoril dvere voliéry a udrel si hlavu o rám dverí.

Niekedy sme sa naozaj dobre zabavili; len dúfam, že ma nezahluší, keď bude čítať v poslednej kapitole o incidente s hadicou. Preukázali obrovskú trpezlivosť a láskavosť cudzincovi v čase, keď to najviac potreboval. To je niečo, na čo nikdy nezabudnem. To ukazuje zároveň, aké fantastické je sokoliarstvo – práca s orlami v Európe.

Ľubo je usilovný a hrdý muž; strávil som s ním veľa dní v lese ťahaním stromov dolu zradnými svahmi, ktoré by zvládli len odvážlivci, a tí, ktorí riskujú. Jeho traktor by bol súci skôr do múzea, no aj tak, on bol schopný šoférovať s ním do svahov kopcov, kam by sa iní neodvážili. Niekedy nútil mňa a ešte jedného kamaráta sedieť vpredu na traktore a pridal ešte nejakú záťaž dopredu, kým on šoféroval hore šmykľavou horskou cestou len na zadných kolesách - aj kaskadér sa môže schovať - nikdy ste nič také nerobili v porovnaní s rizikom, ktoré tento chlapík berie na seba každý deň, okrem servírovania jedla na stôl.

Nech naše priateľstvo prekvitá dlho. Ďakujem ešte raz za úžasnú pohostinnosť, ktorú ste mi preukázali a dovolili mi „zažiť svoj sen" a dosiahnuť svoj cieľ – chytiť slovenského zajaca s Kaiserom.

Váš veľký kamarát

Thomas Carnihan

Books

Falconry & Hawking

"I highly recommend this book, but not under the circumstances by which I acquired it!"

In this **third** edition of his classic guide to training, caring for, and hunting with falcons and hawks, Phillip Glasier, an experienced teacher of falconry, continues to provide the best, most detailed information available to the beginner. In conjunction with raptor specialist Greg Simpson, he presents completely new, fully up-to-date coverage of health and disease, as well in-depth advice on keeping birds of prey

Author Phillip Glasier

Edition 3, illustrated, reprint Publisher Batsford, 2006 ISBN 0713484071, 9780713484076 Falconry & Hawking

Hawking with Golden Eagles

Martin Hollinshead ISBN 0-88839-343-1

This book, based on practical experience, is a must have for all serious Golden Eagle trainers. Giving reference to hunting procedures, when attending eagle meetings. Although I've never met Martin Hollinshead I find his book is extremely well written, and clearly he knows his subject better than most. He talks a lot of common sense and it's evident upon reading the book that here is a man who not only writes well but has also spent a great deal of time in the field, and has learnt his craft well. The only disappointment is the book's format. To do it justice I feel it should have been published in hardback. This is only a minor criticism as this book on hunting with Golden Eagles is well worth reading.

This is an account of one man's 30-year involvement with England's rarest bird, the golden eagle. Initially employed by the RSPB as a senior species protection warden at a secret location in Cumbria, the author describes the intricacies of establishing a protection regime by wardens that would operate for the next 26 years and his efforts to protect and study this iconic species. The Lakeland eagles were at their most productive during his tenure, rearing six eaglets in the six years before he widened his interest to study eagles in Scotland as well as England. The author discovered and recorded many previously unknown facts about golden eagles. He began to plan and implement projects which would expand knowledge of the species as well as helping to secure their foothold in England. His project is the most detailed and complete study of a pair of golden eagles with, at its heart, the life and times of an eagle he followed from its arrival in 1982 until its death, 22 years later. A bird that would eventually show little fear of him and accept his presence rather than flee. The author recounts the hardships experienced by the eagle and eagle-watcher alike, and his record of behaviour at the nest is unparalleled. However, working with golden eagles is not without difficulties and the author's encounters with unsympathetic shepherds and poor decision-making are also described, as are his dealings with egg collectors who craved to add the rare English eagle eggs to their collections. His efforts to counter their intrusions even saw him rebuilding eagle eyries that had been so dispassionately destroyed! However, "Call of the Eagle" amply illustrates the close attachment and passion that drove the author to devote so much of his life to this magnificent raptor, famed as the King of Birds.

ACKNOWLEDGEMENTS

Having left school more years ago than I care to remember and coming away with a report that said "needs to learn to read and write and spend less time wagging school to go fishing;" I often wondered where did I go wrong? Forty five years later I have finally learnt to read and write, thank God for things like spell check! The sense of achievement in writing a book through all the adversity that's been thrown at me over the last several years is indescribable, I'm thrilled to bits that it's now finished. However I must give special thanks to my falconry friends who have allowed me to photograph their hawks and eagles, without their help the book wouldn't be in print. Also to a great friend, Teresa Akgunduz, who has tirelessly put up with my late night calls and text, asking if it reads ok? And why can't I say lol? instead of Ha Ha! Without her proof reading skills and patience again it wouldn't be in print. Special thanks to Terry in Swindon (Frick, to her friends) and Bob who helped enormously in getting my website www.where eagles hare.com up and running.

To Bob Watkins, close friend and falconer, who is also a very talented graphic designer and who helped me with technical assistance and again a big thank you for putting up with the constant flood of emails with " how do I do this?" and his witty text replies like "CAN'T TALK NOW I'M IN SPAIN" or "Give me ten and I'll ring you back" which sometimes meant ten days, lol! And "You sure this can't go there?" (widows and orphans for the writers amongst you.)

Big thank you to Kirsten Rohloff, an excellent amateur photographer friend on Facebook, from Germany. Who has been giving me lessons over the internet on photography. People say my photos are stunning, well I really don't know anything about photography, I just point and shoot! Now I'm quite sure with Kirsten's help my photos will be so much better. Also a big thank you to all my facebook friends, including cousin William (Carnihan) Susan Ann Watt, Denise Gatliffe, Lemay's Renee, Lorraine Bondi and to all you others who regulary comment on my photos, many many thanks.

And last but no means least a very special thank you to Elizabeth Edwards who made me believe in myself and gave me enormous encouragement to write this book about Kaiscr and gave me the strength to go on and rebuild my life. At times when I struggled and couldn't talk to others you were always there to listen and offer help and guidance, thank you so much.

95% of the photo's in the book were taken by myself and the vast majority of those were taken using only one hand as I had Kaiser on my fist if he wasn't in the actual photo.

Several photos in the book have been sent to me via Facebook, from friends who do not know who took original photo of them, thank you.

Page 19 Hugh Miles

Page 21 (Bottom left) Mark Thacker

Page 31 Lubo Engler

Page 83 John Mease and friends

Page 84 Josef Hiebeler

Page 153 "Pitbull"

Page 161 (Bottom Right) friends of Roxanne Peggie

Page 178 Gerrit Kulik

Page 194 Friends of Keith Davies

Page 217 Middle photo of hare, Kirsten Rohloff

Page 247—249 Viktor Wercholák

Back cover Photograph Robert and Peter Howgego's farm Nordelph, Norfolk

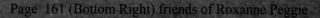

255

Chlapci sú späť v meste